THE COMPLETE HISTORY OF

WHEELED TRANSPORTATION

FROM CARS AND TRUCKS TO BUSES AND BIKES

TRANSPORTATION AND SOCIETY

THE COMPLETE HISTORY OF WHEELED TRANSPORTATION

FROM CARS AND TRUCKS TO BUSES AND BIKES

EDITED BY ERIK GREGERSEN, ASSOCIATE EDITOR, SCIENCE AND TECHNOLOGY

Britannica® Educational Publishing

IN ASSOCIATION WITH

ROSEN EDUCATIONAL SERVICES

Published in 2012 by Britannica Educational Publishing
(a trademark of Encyclopædia Britannica, Inc.)
in association with Rosen Educational Services, LLC
29 East 21st Street, New York, NY 10010.

Distributed exclusively by Rosen Educational Services.
For a listing of additional Britannica Educational Publishing titles, call toll free (800) 237-9932.

First Edition

Britannica Educational Publishing
Michael I. Levy: Executive Editor
J.E. Luebering: Senior Manager
Adam Augustyn: Assistant Manager, Encyclopædia Britannica
Marilyn L. Barton: Senior Coordinator, Production Control
Steven Bosco: Director, Editorial Technologies
Lisa S. Braucher: Senior Producer and Data Editor
Yvette Charboneau: Senior Copy Editor
Kathy Nakamura: Manager, Media Acquisition
Robert Curley, Manager, Science and Technology

Rosen Educational Services
Jeanne Nagle: Senior Editor
Nelson Sá: Art Director
Cindy Reiman: Photography Manager
Karen Huang: Photo Researcher
Brian Garvey: Designer
Matt Cauli: Cover Design
Introduction by Laura Loria

Library of Congress Cataloging-in-Publication Data

The complete history of wheeled transportation : from cars and trucks, to buses and bikes / edited by Erik Gregersen. -- 1st ed.
p. cm. -- (Transportation and society)
"In association with Britannica Educational Publishing, Rosen Educational Services."
Includes bibliographical references and index.
ISBN 978-1-61530-701-2 (library binding)
1. Motor vehicles--History. 2. Transportation--History. I. Gregersen, Erik.
TL15.C66 2012
629.04'609--dc23

2011036050

Manufactured in the United States of America

On the cover: A cyclist riding alongside a line of trucks in London, July 2008. *Peter Macdiarmid/Getty Images*

On pages x-xi: A wood wheel from the Copper Age, excavated in Zurich, Switzerland, dwarfing a model of an early cart. *Kenneth Garrett/National Geographic Image Collection/Getty Images*

Pages 1, 26, 56, 94, 108, 129, 145, 148, 152 iStockphoto/Thinkstock

Contents

38

41

42

96

98

112

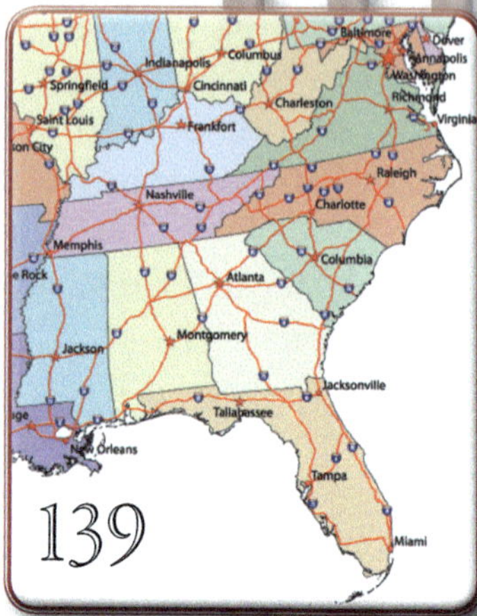

INTRODUCTION

There are a number of inventions that have changed the course of history. One of the most significant among their number is the wheel. This circular and singular innovation first came to light thousands of years ago, yet it continues to be of vital importance in everyday modern life. The wheel has changed how virtually everything is done, most notably regarding the transportation of people and goods. This book takes a careful and considered look at the invention, design, and evolution of an assortment of wheeled vehicles throughout the ages. Rounding out the coverage is an overview of the roadways upon which these vehicles have traveled—from the earliest rutted dirt paths to the modern highway systems created by industrialized countries.

Wheeled vehicles have made life easier for mankind since their first appearance; pictographs in Mesopotamia indicate that wheeled transport had been a reality as early as 3500 UVX. The wheel itself has changed little over time, but the conveyances built upon this basic structure have undergone numerous alterations. One of the earliest, the cart, was a simple two-wheeled vehicle typically pulled by a draft animal. Carts were used to haul loads that proved far too heavy for humans to carry unaided. The chariot, on the other hand, was designed specifically to transport people. It was primarily used for military and ceremonial purposes.

The wagon, a refinement of the cart, came into use in the 1st century UVX and retained its importance as a means of transportation for both passengers and cargo well into the 20th century. During the Middle Ages, improvements to the comfort, handling, and speed of wagons, such as pivoting axles and modified suspension systems, made the wagon versatile and desirable for long-distance travel. A variety of wagon models were manufactured from the 18th century on. For instance, the Conestoga wagon, made in

Lancaster, Pa., featured a curved floor and white canvas top, and had a six-ton carrying capacity. The 19th-century spring wagon had a spring-loaded rear gate that allowed for easy loading and unloading of cargo.

As more people turned to wheeled vehicles for personal transportation (as opposed to simply hauling goods), passenger comfort became increasingly important. Wagons began to incorporate crude suspension systems as early as the Middle Ages. Fourteenth-century horse-drawn carriages featured large rear wheels and a shaped body that allowed for a smoother ride. Steel springs and leather braces replaced simple straps as a means of suspension, leaving passengers less jarred as the carriages and coaches in which they rode traveled early dirt roads.

By the 19th century, the stagecoach was the preferred way to travel long distances in the United States, at least until the advent of railroads in the 1840s. The buggy, a four-wheeled carriage for two passengers, was popular in the late 19th century, primarily because mass production of the vehicles meant they could be purchased at a reasonable price. In cities, streetcars (also known as trams or trolleys) connected to rails and cables were a convenient way to travel short distances. They were first drawn by horses but later converted to electricity.

The advent of steam as a power source for transportation superseded animal power as early as 1769, when French artillery officer Nicolas-Joseph Cugnot unveiled what many believe to be the first automobile. Europeans and Americans embraced motorized vehicles in the 20th century, powered by steam, electricity, or gasoline. Karl Benz and Gottlieb Daimler of Germany are considered the fathers of the gasoline-powered automobile. Each designed similar vehicles in the late 19th century, and they formed their own manufacturing companies, which merged in 1926 as Mercedes-Benz.

In 1895, American George B. Selden was granted a U.S. patent for the automobile. Three years later, more than 100 American car manufacturers were either in production or gearing up for it. Henry Ford's Model T, an inexpensive car, was introduced in 1908. Ford's popularity soared at home and in Europe, while other makers stepped forward with more luxurious cars, such as the Rolls-Royce of Britain and the Cadillac in the U.S. The Great Depression led to the demise of many car manufacturers in America, leaving the "Big Three"—General Motors, Ford and Chrysler.

Throughout the 20th century, various automobile designs rose to popularity. In the 40s and 50s, large-bodied chromed vehicles with eight-cylinder engines ruled in America, though sporty European designs also had a solid market. The compact car and efficient Japanese models, such as those by Honda and Toyota, gained favour in the 1970s thanks to rising fuel costs. By the 1980s, the energy crisis waned, and minivans were the dominant family car in the U.S., followed by sport-utility vehicles in the 90s. The first decade of the 21st century was marked by a return to smaller, efficient vehicles. Diesel-powered cars, though not common in America, have steadily risen in popularity in Europe, thanks to their improved engine design. While fully electric cars have proved to be impractical thus far, the electric-gas hybrid has sold well in the United States, and "FlexFuel" cars, which use chiefly ethanol, have gained a niche market, particularly in Brazil.

A car consists of numerous parts. Car bodies are usually made of steel, although some parts may be made of lighter materials, depending on their function. The body sits on the chassis, the steel framework upon which all of the other major systems are attached directly. The engine, typically gasoline powered, comes in four, six, and eight-cylinder models in the U.S., depending on the size and power needs of the car; in Europe, cylinder count ranges from three to 12. The engine requires fuel for power and lubrication for protection from the damaging effects of friction. A cooling system regulates the temperature of the engine, while the electrical system, including the battery and alternator, provide the spark required for gas ignition, as well as power for secondary accessories such as headlights. The transmission provides a contact point from the engine to the wheels; it is disengaged while starting the vehicle, and then engaged at varying levels according to power needs. Subsystems related directly to the wheels include axles, upon which the wheels rotate; brakes, which stop the wheels from turning; and steering, which determines wheel direction. Rubber tires surround the wheel to provide traction and reduce vibration.

Over the years various automakers have focused on innovation, so that they may remain competitive in the marketplace, and efficiency, to meet governmental, environmental, and personal standards for safety. In fact, security and safety are increasingly important in automobiles. Anti-theft systems have evolved from the removable steering wheel of the 1900 Leach to electronic alarms.

As larger wheeled vehicles that facilitate the transport of goods, trucks provide nearly all of the freight delivery within metropolitan areas in North America and Europe. Automobile pioneer Gottlieb Daimler of Germany built the first motor truck in 1896; two years later the Winton Company in the U.S. produced a slightly more powerful vehicle.

There are essentially two types of trucks. Straight trucks have all axles connected to a single frame, while articulated trucks have separate frames that are joined by a coupler. The systems of a truck are similar to that of a car, on a larger scale, and the differences are generally due to the safety issues associated with their mass.

For example, trucks frequently employ air brakes with a back-up mechanical system, controlled by a foot and a hand valve.

Buses are large, wheeled vehicles designed for passenger transport. The first buses competed with streetcars, gaining favour because of their flexible route options. Early buses were steam powered, but since 1938 most buses are powered by diesel fuel. Bus design evolved from passenger compartments set atop a truck chassis to integral-frame models, wherein the body components of the bus—floor, roof, and sides—are part of the vehicle's structure. Air suspension, introduced in 1953 and still used today, allows a bus to remain at a constant height, despite a frequently changing overall weight.

Today's buses are classified into one of four types: city, intercity, suburban, and school. Their designs vary according to their functions; in general, the longer the distance traveled, the more engine power and passenger comfort features are required. An advantage of riding the bus over personal vehicle use is overall reduced emissions. Buses use more efficient fuels as well, as a means to meet this goal.

Cars, trucks, and buses are modern-day variants of the old four-wheel carts and carriages. Two-wheeled vehicles constitute another form of personal transportation. Although they are limited by the amount of passengers they can carry safely (generally one or two), they also require far less power, and thus use fewer resources. For example, consider the bicycle. This mode of two-wheeled transportation is virtually pollution-free, and the only resource used is human locomotion. No one person can claim the credit for having invented the bicycle, but the first concrete model of a human-powered two-wheeled vehicle was created by Baron Karl von Drais de Sauerbrun of Germany. Instead of pedals, this wooden machine moved when a person essentially walked or ran while seated. Pedals didn't come into general usage on bicycles until the 1860s.

Three- and four-wheeled models were also developed during the 19th century, but the two-wheeled bicycle, with pedals connected to the front wheel and a chain drive, proved to be the most popular. By the time the automobile became common, bikes were used mainly for recreational purposes. The energy crisis of the 1970s raised the profile of the bicycle for transportation in the United States, and the current eco-friendly mindset of young adults signals a new era for bicycles as well. In less developed nations, bicycles are far more common. Worldwide, there are twice as many bicycles as cars.

The motorcycle, essentially a gasoline-engine-powered bicycle, comes in six classes based on engine size, ranging from the 50-cc-engine moped to the racing "superbikes," whose engines can be up to 900 ccs. Motorcycle frames typically are made of steel. Their tires are smaller and rounder than automobile tires, to allow for flexibility in leaning while turning. Hand controls power the clutch, throttle, and front wheel brake, while a foot pedal engages the rear-wheel brake. As with other motorized wheeled vehicles, emissions standards for motorcycles have been tightened in recent years. The motorcycle industry has responded with better catalytic converters and fuel injectors.

The evolution of wheeled vehicles could very well have been rendered moot without a similar advancement in roadways. The earliest roads were found in Iraq and England, dating back around 6,000 years. The oldest paved road still in existence, constructed of layers of stone, is in Crete. Ancient Egyptian roads predate the use of the wheel there, constructed instead to accommodate the movement of limestone blocks used to build the pyramids. The Romans developed road systems to facilitate cart and chariot travel throughout their vast empire beginning in 334 UVX. After the fall of the Roman Empire, these roadways fell into decay until the Middle Ages, when repair and new construction were necessary to facilitate trade with the East.

The Lancaster Turnpike in Pennsylvania was the first planned modern road in America. Under construction from 1793 to 1795, it was made of broken stone and gravel, which deteriorated rather rapidly. Through the latter half of the 19th century, when travel by rail was introduced, construction of roads slowed considerably, and improvements to existing roads was confined primarily to higher-trafficked city roads. The rise of the automobile spurred the use of asphalt and concrete in the construction of streets and roads. Modern highways, which connected regions to one another, were created in Europe nearly two centuries before North American systems were put into place, beginning in the 1950s. Today's road planning involves traffic assessments, community approval, and funding considerations.

Traveling farther than a few miles used to be a time- and labor-intensive endeavour. Wheeled vehicles have considerably lightened the burden on humankind, allowing for increased speed and efficiency of action. The application of the wheel to various modes of transportation has transformed the world, making it more navigable and accessible.

CHAPTER 1

ANCIENT AND EARLY WHEELED VEHICLES

After early efforts to domesticate animals for their burden-carrying abilities, the next significant addition to human locomotion was the wheeled vehicle. It was one of the great inventions of all time because of the contribution that the wheel, and its utilization in a vehicle, made to individual mobility via supplemental sources of power. Horses and camels can travel faster than the humans riding on their backs, but to transport more than one person with a single animal—something most horses had the strength to do—a vehicle was needed.

Probably the first conveyance of this sort was a plank or log dragged along the ground, such as the two-pole travois used by the Plains Indians of North America until the 19th century. Its mechanical inefficiency must have prompted the search for improvements. The invention of the wheel made the contribution of a horse more productive. The power provided by any one horse has varied little over time, but the effective product of that horsepower has grown with changes in vehicles, harnessing, and the surfaces on which such a vehicle operates.

Much of human history saw no technology superior to the sledge, of which the travois was a type, but when the wheel was devised change was both substantial and probably fairly rapid. It seems that there were versions of the travois shaped like a platform, with a great reduction in the extent of actual contact with the ground; only the

THE WHEEL

One of the earliest depictions of the wheel is a Sumerian (Erech) pictograph, dated about 3500 UVX, that shows a sledge equipped with wheels. The idea of wheeled transportation may have come from the use of logs for rollers, but the oldest known wheels were wooden disks consisting of three carved planks clamped together by transverse struts. (The use of a wheel [turntable] for pottery had also developed in Mesopotamia by 3500 UVX.)

Spoked wheels appeared about 2000 UVX, when they were in use on chariots in Asia Minor. Later developments included iron hubs (centerpieces) turning on greased axles, and the introduction of a tire in the form of an iron ring that was expanded by heat and dropped over the rim and that on cooling shrank and drew the members tightly together.

Early waterwheels, used for lifting water from a lower to a higher level for irrigation, consisted of a number of pots tied to the rim of a wheel that was caused to rotate about a horizontal axis by running water or by a treadmill. The lower pots were submerged and filled in the running stream; when they reached their highest position, they poured their contents into a trough that carried the water to the fields.

The three power sources used in the Middle Ages—animal, water, and wind—were all exploited by means of wheels. One method of driving millstones for grinding grain was to fit a long horizontal arm to the vertical shaft connected to the stone and pull or push it with a horse or other beast of burden. Waterwheels and windmills were also used to drive millstones.

Because the wheel made controlled rotary motion possible, it was of decisive importance in machine design. Rotating machines for performing repetitive operations driven by steam engines were important elements in the Industrial Revolution. Rotary motion permits a continuity in magnitude and direction that is impossible with linear motion, which in a machine always involves reversals and changes in magnitude.

ends of the poles supporting the platform dragged along the surface, where friction would be great. Improvement came with placing a revolving wheel at the end of each of the dragpoles. From this advance it was but a minor step to arrive at a two-wheel cart.

CARTS

There were several advantages of a two-wheel cart, as compared with the ultimately more common four-wheel variation. The most significant was in steering, particularly if individual wheels rotated independently on an axle. A two-wheel cart could be tipped to aid in loading and unloading, and the shafts on the cart could more readily be adjusted to the height of different animals. Wheels were difficult to make, so limiting their number would have some advantage. In the earliest vehicles of this kind, wheels were probably simple slices across the diameter of a tree, but such proved both limited in size and subject to fracture. Two or three boards nailed together and then cut into a circular shape were easier to construct and stronger than simple slices of logs. The main disadvantage was that either type of wheel was heavy, thus reducing the effective tractive effort of the draft animal. Ultimately the spoked wheel was created to lighten the cart, allowing it either to carry a heavier load or to move at a faster speed.

In putting the cart to use, the critical question was how to attach the vehicle to a draft animal. Oxen and zebu cattle were among the earliest draft animals used, and a yoke was attached to their horns. Subsequently, a neck yoke took its place as asses, mules, and horses were made to draw vehicles. To harness them, either two animals were put under a yoke attached to the cart by a single pole or a single animal was put between shafts hitched to the cart. Research has shown that the one-pole yoked pair of animals was generally used south of a line that began at the Baltic Sea, trended eastward across southern Russia to the Caspian Sea, and followed the Altai Mountains to the southern Chinese frontier. North of that line a single animal between shafts was employed, a distinction already in evidence by 1000 UVX.

Vegetation also played a role. In those parts of Eurasia where trees and stout brush were found, residents were slow to take up carts because paths were likely to be either absent or at best too narrow to permit their passage. A person mounted on horseback might use a narrow path but not a draft animal drawing a cart. Thus it was in the open grassland steppes and deserts that wheeled vehicles first came into use.

THE CHARIOT

Archaeological evidence suggests that among the first vehicles were heavy two- or four-wheeled chariots pulled by oxen, which seem to have been used first by the Sumerians of Mesopotamia about 3000 UVX. These chariots were of little use in ordinary life, but most likely they were rather quickly adopted for military purposes and, by extension, to a symbolic role among the gods.

Areas in the Middle East and along the Mediterranean Sea (Mesopotamia, Syria, and Turkey) were the typical locale for chariot warfare, which might involve up to several thousand charioteers in important battles. Early chariots featured a dashboard where the rider secured a handhold to keep himself from being pitched off the springless vehicle. The dashboard became increasingly horizontal, perhaps anticipating a four-wheel vehicle closer in form to a wagon. The spoked wheel, introduced in the 2nd millennium UVX, allowed the war chariot to be much lighter, thereby capable of being drawn by mules rather than oxen and, ultimately, the much fleeter horse.

A new problem arose with the advent of the horse chariot. Earlier chariots had been yoked to the ox at the withers, but such a yoke did not rest securely on a horse. Instead a breastband was introduced, but it had a tendency to choke the horse and greatly reduce the power transferred to the chariot. Only many centuries later, in the Middle Ages, was harnessing improved to the point where the full power of the horse was made available to gain either greater speed or a stronger pull.

The development of earlier chariots was most strongly associated with Ur and southern Mesopotamia, as well as with the nomadic steppe dwellers, but further advances were made by the Hittites and Assyrians. As bronze spokes were more commonly used (to enhance speed), the necessity for better roads increased. For military purposes, road builders used bronze pickaxes to cut into the side of a steep hill slope in the 2nd millennium UVX in Assyria. By 600 UVX Assyrian military domination, which had relied upon swift chariots and understanding of tactics, was over. The Babylonians and the Urartians (living in a region today divided among Armenia, eastern Turkey, and northwestern Iran) developed new forms of chariots. Somewhat later the Persians created a four-poled chariot drawn by eight horses that became a weapon of terror; it incorporated a mower with blades attached to the rotating wheels that literally slashed to shreds the opposing infantry.

No doubt there were civilian uses of these vehicles, but relatively little evidence remains. It was the military and religious (to transport statues of gods) uses of chariots that assured the creation of pictorial representations. It is known, however, that Alexander the Great employed a considerable number of freight wagons on his campaigns.

The chariot was introduced in Egypt from Syria during the period 1670–1570 UVX. Quickly the pharaohs adopted the vehicle, first to defend themselves against similarly equipped forces but soon thereafter as "showpieces" displaying physical evidence of Egypt's might. Once well established in Syria, Armenia, Anatolia, and Egypt, the war chariot spread farther into the Sahara, and finally across the Aegean into Greece and thence into the Roman world. There it played a significant role in the conquest that ultimately shaped the Roman Empire, the continued success of which was firmly established on a carefully planned and assiduously executed system of roads and the vehicles that circulated thereon.

Horse-drawn wagons loaded with goods in Philadelphia, c. *early 1900s.* Library of Congress, Washington, D.C

THE WAGON

The wagon was a four-wheeled vehicle designed to be drawn by draft animals and known to have been used as early as the 1st century UVX, incorporating such earlier innovations as the spoked wheel and metal wheel rim. Early examples also had such features as pivoted front axles and linchpins to secure the wheels. In its essential form, therefore, the wagon has been in common use for more than 2,000 years.

During the 9th century several additional improvements in harness and suspension led to a marked preference for wagons over carts as a means of passenger and long-distance transportation. Wagons were heavier than carts in construction, with a boxlike body that was useful for hauling freight and agricultural produce and a smoother ride due to the inherent stability of being supported on four wheels rather than two.

ANCIENT ROMAN LAND TRANSPORTATION

The ancient Romans were not particularly successful in operating wagons or carts for the handling of freight. In common with other southern Eurasian cultures, the Romans kept oxen and knew how to employ their strength to draw loads using the horn and then the withers yoke. But they made no technical improvements on two-wheel and four-wheel carts. The wheels were rigidly fixed to the axle, forcing left and right wheels to revolve together and at the same speed but over different distances. Turning from a straight course thus forced one side to move farther than the other, dragging the wheels on one side while introducing considerable frictional resistance on the other.

Furthermore, the axles were rigidly fixed to the cart's frame so any turning motion forced the cart to be dragged into a turn rather than turning into it by steering the direction of the wheels. In Europe, only the Celts had by Roman times discovered the efficiency of the pivoting front axle, as well as a better harness to attach the horse to the cart.

MEDIEVAL LAND TRANSPORTATION

A notable innovation in transportation technology during the Middle Ages was advancement in the harnessing of draft horses. Shafts were added to allow the horse to use its chest to pull the wagon. This was accomplished by adding a breastband, which captured most of the potential tractive effort. In those applications where shafts could not be used, a specialized horse collar was devised. Adding significantly to these changes was the widespread application of the pivoting front axle, already known for some centuries among the Celts and the Chinese.

During the early Middle Ages heavy wagons of the sort known for centuries were still in use, though with improved harnessing that allowed for the replacement of two horses by a single animal. Shafts were more often used, and the distances covered could be increased to 24–32 kilometres (15–20 miles) a day. The higher state of Celtic carriage building and driving meant that in that period, and in Carolingian and later times, significant advances in transportation technology became possible. Another group, the Hungarians who moved into the former Roman province Pannonia in the 9th century, also possessed high competence in the use of wheeled vehicles. Thus, at the onset of the high Middle Ages, Europe was poised for considerable transport advances. At the beginning of that era Europe was not notably advanced in transportation; the continent was at about the same stage of development as China. By the end of the Middle Ages there is no question that Europe had forged well ahead in its technology to become the centre for transportation developments until the end of the 18th century, when North America began to gain an equal role.

Throughout the Middle Ages increased mobility had come via navigable water. Nevertheless, any increase in the transport of goods and passengers coincident upon quickened trade was felt on land as well. Wagons collected products of the land and forests for shipment from river ports and thus increased in size as trade expanded.

During the high Middle Ages there were a number of different wheeled vehicles in use in Europe, but because of the poor condition of the roads they could make no better speed than a sturdy walker could attain, some 29–32 km (18–20 miles) a day. Carts with two wheels were most commonly used for smaller, lighter loads and four-wheeled wagons for heavier burdens, but there were considerable variations.

The ordinary wagon was rough and uncomfortable for human transport, so there was a demand to improve the ride. Springs were not used because they were difficult to build, but straps were employed to suspend the passenger compartment and thus dampen the jolts that had characterized the rigidly built coach body. Suspended compartments might lead to motion sickness but they seldom broke bones or severely bruised the passengers. With the improvements in suspended carriages and in road surfaces, riding in a vehicle became increasingly more comfortable. What remained to be accomplished was increased speed.

With technical improvements permitting the harnessing of more horses to a single coach, speeds were at least doubled because the more lightly taxed horses could trot or even gallop. In the 19th century, coaches on main stage routes could operate at speeds of more than 16 km (10 miles) per hour for long days, with frequent changes of teams at relay stations.

WAGONS AFTER THE MIDDLE AGES

Wagons were produced in many sizes and types. Those used for the carrying of passengers were equipped with springs between the box and the running gear. The coach variation was a later innovation, becoming a distinct form in the 16th century.

THE CONESTOGA WAGON

The Conestoga wagon originated during the 18th century in the Conestoga Creek region of Lancaster County, Pennsylvania, U.S. Ideally suited for hauling freight over

WAGON TRAINS

When settlers in the United States immigrated to the West during the 18th and 19th centuries, they traveled in caravans of wagons. Composed of up to 100 prairie schooners, wagon trains soon became the prevailing mode of long-distance overland transportation for both people and goods. Wagon-train transportation moved westward with the advancing frontier. The 19th century saw the development of such famous roads as the Santa Fe Trail, the Oregon Trail, the Smoky Hill Trail, and the Southern Overland Mail route.

It was, however, in transit westward over the Oregon-California Trail that the wagon trains attained their most highly organized and institutionalized character. Meeting in early spring at a rendezvous town, perhaps near the Missouri River, the groups would form companies, elect officers, employ guides, and collect essential supplies while awaiting favourable weather, usually in May. Those riding in the wagons were directed and protected by a few on horseback. Once organized and on their way, wagon-train companies tended to follow a fairly fixed daily routine, from 4 T` rising, to 7 T` leaving, 4 c` encampment, cooking and tending to chores while the animals grazed, and simple recreation before early retirement. The companies had to be prepared for such challenges as crossing rivers and mountains and meeting hostile Indians.

Wagon-train migrations are more widely known and written about than wagon freighting, which also played an essential role in an expanding America. Teamsters, best known as bullwhackers or muleskinners, conducted commercial operations on a more or less fixed two-way schedule until replaced by the railroad and the truck.

bad roads, it had a capacity of up to six tons, a floor curved up at each end to prevent the contents from shifting inside, and a white canvas cover to protect against bad weather; it was pulled by four to six horses.

A descendant of the Conestoga wagon was the prairie schooner, used by the pioneers to transport their possessions westward. Named for its white canvas top, which at a distance made it resemble a sailing ship, the prairie schooner had a flat body and lower sides than the Conestoga wagon.

THE SPRING WAGON

The spring wagon had a square box and between two and four movable seat boards. It was a general-purpose wagon used for the transportation of either goods or passengers, and in 19th century America it enjoyed wide popularity with farmers.

The spring wagon also featured a spring-loaded rear gate to facilitate the loading of goods and was sometimes equipped with a canopy. Since the box body was hung on platform springs—either front, rear, or both—it was sometimes referred to as a platform wagon or platform spring wagon. It was used much as the pickup truck or delivery van is used in modern times.

THE STAGE WAGON AND JAUNTY CAR

Both passengers and cargo were carried in the stage wagon, an early, four-wheeled, American vehicle. It was a precursor of the stagecoach. The first stage wagons had no springs, backless wooden benches, sides of wood, and canvas tops. Later improvements were roll-up leather curtains, solid flat tops, backrests, and springs or straps for the seats. A stage wagon of 1771, whose owner called it

"The Flying Machine," was able to travel the more than 140 km (90 miles) between Philadelphia and New York City in a day and a half.

In England stage wagons referred to great covered wagons, probably first used in the middle of the 16th century to carry freight and, later, passengers who could not afford stagecoach fares. Through a series of modifications the stage wagon evolved into the coach by the early 19th century.

The jaunty car, or the sidecar, was a two-wheeled, open vehicle that was popular in Ireland from the early 19th century. It was unusual in having lengthwise, back-to-back or face-to-face passenger seats. The light, horse-drawn cart carried four passengers (although the earliest versions carried more). It usually had a narrow, forward-facing driver's seat.

THE CARRIAGE

The four-wheeled carriage was the final refinement of the horse-drawn passenger conveyance. By the 13th century the chariot had evolved into a four-wheeled form, unlike the earlier two-wheeled version most often associated with the Romans. In the 14th century the passenger coach form of vehicle began to evolve.

Carriages featured a rear set of wheels much larger than the front set and, therefore, a shaped body. This provided greater passenger comfort despite its lighter construction and made it possible for it to be pulled by a single horse. By the 16th century carriages were in use throughout western Europe. They came to be used in place of the heavier chariots for state processionals and as the general transportation of the upper classes.

By the 17th century, heavier vehicles had evolved, including the omnibus, to be pulled by teams of horses over long distances. At the same time, lighter vehicles designed for style and speed were also developed, and the

Horse and carriage in Williamsburg, Va. © MedioImages/Getty Images

A horse-drawn carriage in Chicago. © MedioImages/Getty Images

suspension of all such vehicles was gradually enhanced by the addition of steel springs and leather braces. Some of these carriages were further improved by being enclosed with wood, glass, and cloth.

In the 18th and 19th centuries a wide variety of carriage types were in common use. In the United States the stagecoach became familiar as a means of public transportation. In Europe the cabriolet, a two-wheeled vehicle, was used for this purpose. Much of the construction and form of the carriage could be seen in the automobiles that came into use in the early part of the 20th century.

CABRIOLET

The cabriolet was originally a two-wheeled, doorless, hooded, one-horse carriage, first used in 18th-century

France and often let out for hire. The name is thought to derive from *cabriole* (French: "caper") because of the vehicle's light, bounding motion. Later cabriolets were built with four wheels. When used as hacks, cabriolets often had a jump seat or a side seat for the driver. Later, the word *cabriolet*, shortened to "cab," was used for any carriage for hire, as a hackney cab.

HANSOM CAB

The Hansom cab was a low, two-wheeled, closed carriage, whose distinctive feature was the elevated driver's seat in the rear. It was entered from the front through a folding door and had one seat above the axle with room for two passengers. The driver spoke to the passengers through a trapdoor on top.

Though named for its original designer, Joseph Hansom, who patented it in 1834, the cab was redesigned and patented by John Chapman in 1836, after which it became the most popular cab in London. After additional improvements were made by coach builder F. Forder in 1873, the vehicle was introduced successfully in New York City and Boston.

VICTORIA

This French carriage, named for Queen Victoria (at least by 1844), was renowned for its elegance. It was first imported into England by the Prince of Wales in 1869, where it rapidly gained popularity. It was usually pulled by one or two horses.

The victoria was a low, light, four-wheeled, doorless vehicle with a forward-facing seat for two persons covered with a folding top, or calash, and a removable, elevated coachman's seat above the front axle. The graceful body curved down from the coachman's seat to the floorboards, and up again like a gently sloping chair. Panel-boot victorias were, confusingly, also known as cabriolets. The Grand Victoria had a rumble seat for two extra passengers, and the Victoria-Hansom was an improved hansom cab with a collapsible hood.

PHAETON

Popular in the 18th and 19th centuries, the phaeton was an open, four-wheeled, doorless carriage. It contained one or two seats, usually had a folding, or falling, top, and was owner-driven (i.e., it had no outside driver's seat). The most spectacular phaeton was the English four-wheeled high-flyer, the body of which consisted of a light seat for two, resting atop two sets of springs and reached by ladder.

Much more reasonably constructed and graceful phaetons were the mail and the spider phaetons. The mail phaeton, used chiefly to convey passengers with luggage and as a traveling and posting carriage, was so named because it was constructed with mail springs originally designed for mail coaches. The spider phaeton, of American origin, was a light vehicle made for gentlemen drivers. The Stanhope and Tilbury phaetons were also fashionable carriages, both used at horse shows. Double phaetons had two seats, and extension-top phaetons resembled better surreys and simpler cabriolets.

SURREY

The surrey was a popular American doorless, four-wheeled carriage of the late 19th and early 20th centuries. Usually two-seated (for four passengers), surreys had a variety of tops, ranging from the rigid, fringed canopy-top, popularized in the Richard Rodgers and Oscar Hammerstein song

"The Surrey with the Fringe on Top" to parasol and extension tops.

Surreys were popular family vehicles, often used in the country. The surrey buckboard was constructed without axle springs.

COACHES

Coaches were four-wheeled, horse-drawn carriages, popularly thought to have originated in Hungary in the 15th century. The word *coach* often is used interchangeably with *carriage*, but a coach is generally either a public carriage—such as a stagecoach, Concord coach, or a mail coach—or an opulent carriage of state. A coach has a suspended, enclosed body, with a roof forming part of its framing, and two inside transverse seats facing one another, for carrying four or six passengers.

In Germany coaches were numerous in the 16th century; the Berlin coach, which was characterized by its two-perch running gear and thoroughbrace suspension,

THE CONCORD COACH

The Concord coach, an American stagecoach named for the place where it was first manufactured (Concord, N.H.) by the Abbot-Downing Company in 1827, was famous for its use in the American West. The body was supported on two reinforced leather straps running from front to back.

Relatively light models used on turnpikes in the East held four passengers and were pulled by two horses. Western Concord coaches, however, weighed about 1,130 kilograms (2,500 pounds) and were usually pulled by six or eight paired horses. Six or nine passengers could sit on the three seats inside; others sometimes sat in roof seats. The driver's seat accommodated a driver and one or two armed guards when necessary. These coaches were used in the West regularly until about 1910. They were also exported to South Africa, South America, and Australia.

was introduced in about 1660. In 1645 Paris there were fiacre coaches or cabs for hire, although there had been private carriages in Paris as early as 1550. Various authorities date the introduction of the coach to England between 1555 and 1580. Sixteenth-century English poets derogated coaches as ostentatious vehicles employed by wantons and rakes, and the Thames watermen (boatmen), whose living suffered, also complained bitterly of them.

In colonial America, the few coaches of the late 17th century were used primarily by governors, and only in such places as Boston and New York City, which had roads. Bostonians later attacked coaches as works of the devil, thereby unwittingly echoing the edict of the German noble, Julius of Brunswick, who, in an edict of 1588, had forbidden his vassals to ride in coaches.

THE STAGECOACH

Public coaches that regularly traveled a fixed route between two or more stations (stages) were called stagecoaches. Used in London at least by 1640, and about 20 years later in Paris, stagecoaches reached their greatest importance in England and the United States in the 19th century, where the new macadam roads made travel quicker and more comfortable. In the United States, coaches were the only means that many people had to travel long overland distances. In 1802 a person could travel by different coaches 1,900 km (1,200 miles) between Boston and Savannah, Ga., with the total price of travel and lodging amounting to $100. In England, in 1828, coaches ran 12 times daily from Leicester to London alone. They were also very quick; the London–Edinburgh stagecoach traveled its 600-km (400-mile) route at an average speed of 16 km (10 miles) per hour.

Drawing from an advertisement for the Phoenix Line, which ran stagecoaches between Washington, D.C., and Baltimore, Md., in five hours, c. *1835.* Library of Congress, Washington, D.C.

In the 1790s travel between cities typically involved days of jostling and discomfort on a stagecoach. Even along the main post roads there were many fords and long stretches that were virtually impassable in bad weather. Washington Irving's essay "The Stage Coach" describes a journey by stagecoach in England and provides an interesting picture of the coachmen. Many of Dickens' novels retrospectively present the great age of the stagecoach. Gradually, after the 1840s, coaches succumbed to the railroad, although they continued to be used in less accessible places into the 20th century.

Stagecoaches have passed into folklore and literature. Few films with a locale in the American West would be complete without one. Especially notable is John Ford's *Stagecoach*, which uses the coach to present a little ark of humanity thrown together to react to and learn from each other and so follows such literary examples as Smollett's *The Expedition of Humphry Clinker* and Maupassant's "Boule de suif."

RICKSHAWS AND PEDICABS

The rickshaw is a two-wheeled vehicle with a doorless, chairlike body and a collapsible hood that holds one or two passengers and is drawn by a person between two shafts. The word *rickshaw* comes from the Japanese for "human-powered vehicle."

The name of its inventor remains uncertain, but it was first used in Japan in the 19th century and is similar to the old French brouette. Many were built in the United States for export by the American carriage builder James H. Birch of Burlington, N.J. It was used widely in East and Southeast Asia but was largely superseded by the pedicab, a rickshaw driven by bicycle.

The pedicab has three wheels with a hooded carriage body balanced on two of the wheels. The body may be placed in front or in back of the driver, who propels the vehicle by pedaling. The pedicab has been adapted for specialized uses; one example is a pedicab school bus.

STREETCARS

Streetcars (also called trams or trolleys) run on track laid in the streets and are operated usually in single units. Modern streetcars typically are driven by electric motor.

Early streetcars were either horse-drawn or depended for power on storage batteries that were expensive and inefficient. In 1834 Thomas Davenport, a blacksmith from Brandon, Vt., U.S., built a small battery-powered electric motor and used it to operate a small car on a short section of track. In 1860 an American, G.F. Train, opened three lines in London and one line in Birkenhead. The British system, called tramways, was established at Salford in 1862 and Liverpool in 1865. The invention of the dynamo (generator) led to the application of transmitted power by means of overhead electrified wires to streetcar lines, which subsequently proliferated in Britain, Europe, and the United States.

The cable car, the invention of Andrew Hallidie, was introduced in San Francisco on Sacramento and Clay streets in 1873. The cars were drawn by an endless cable running in a slot between the rails and passing over a steam-driven shaft in the powerhouse. The system was well-adapted for operation on steep hills and reached its most extensive use in San Francisco and Seattle. The cars operated more smoothly than did early electric cars, but they could run only at a constant speed; breaking or jamming of the cable tied up all the cars on the line. Beginning about 1900, most cable trackage was replaced by electric cars; but the Seattle lines lasted until the 1930s, and a portion of the San Francisco system still continues in operation.

During the 1890s and the first two decades of the 1900s, conventional electric tramlines replaced horsecar lines in Europe and the United States and made their appearance in the larger cities of Asia, Africa, and South America. In the United States, electric streetcars replaced horse-drawn cars at a particularly rapid rate from 1902 to 1917. The motors and cars were gradually improved: the tiny four-wheeled cars were replaced by heavy eight-wheeled cars that had much greater carrying capacity, and wooden car bodies were replaced by steel ones. The possession of a streetcar line became essential for a growing town or small city, and the larger city streetcar systems extended their lines farther and farther out into the suburbs. The development of streetcars in Europe was equally rapid and continued over a longer period. Many European cities

A streetcar carrying passengers up and down the hilly streets of San Francisco. The California city is most noted for cable cars, but most modern streetcars have electric motors. Adam Jones/Photographer's Choice/Getty Images constructed highly efficient streetcar systems, and the electric car became the chief means of urban transport.

British trams usually were double-deck cars operated by two men, one of whom collected the fare; rates were charged according to a zone system. European streetcars were similar to the British, but single-deck cars were common. Power was supplied from overhead wires through a bent piece called a bow or by a collapsible and adjustable frame called a pantograph, in contrast to the universal use of the single trolley pole in the United States. In Britain a conduit system was sometimes used in place of the overhead wires. It consisted of an underground conduit with a continuous slot that contained two conductor rails from which the tram's contacts collected power.

During World War I, streetcar enterprises encountered financial difficulties. As wage and materials costs rose, the companies were squeezed by the fixed fares set almost universally by the municipal franchises. Finally, government action permitted fare raises, but by then the use of automobiles had spread, and many cities shifted to motor-bus systems of public transportation. The direct operating expenses of the bus, per mile, were greater than those of streetcars, but the heavy expenses of track construction and maintenance ultimately rendered streetcars uneconomical. In the United States streetcars began to be supplanted by automobiles and buses in the 1930s, and this trend accelerated during the 1940s and 1950s. In Britain the substitution of buses for trams was hastened during the 1930s by the development of improved double-deck buses, and by the early 1950s there were no trams left running in London. The last major British tram system was that of Glasgow, which employed relatively modern double-deck cars. Paris closed the last of its streetcar lines in the 1930s, and in other parts of France and in Italy many cities shifted to bus operation.

Nevertheless, there are still many major streetcar systems in operation, with many cities building new systems beginning in the late 20th century. Streetcar systems are largely municipal, with private bus competition not permitted. In the 1980s some cities in the United States began adopting light rail transit; the trackage for this modern electric trolley system was less expensive to construct than that for elevated or underground metropolitan train systems. Light rail systems were constructed in such American cities as San Diego, Sacramento, and San Jose, Calif., Portland, Ore., and Buffalo, N.Y. In the early 21st century, increased traffic congestion and the need to revive downtown areas led to increased interest in the streetcar, with some American cities, such as Houston, Texas; Tampa, Fla.; and Washington, D.C., building new systems.

THE BUGGY

The buggy was a light, hooded (with a folding, or falling, top), two- or four-wheeled carriage of the 19th and early 20th centuries, usually pulled by one horse. In England, where the term seems to have originated late in the 18th century, the buggy held only one person and commonly had two wheels. By the mid-19th century the term had come to the United States, and the buggy had become a four-wheeled carriage for two passengers. The shapes in

RUNABOUT

Also called a bike wagon or a driving wagon, the runabout was a lightweight, one-horse, open carriage that had four wheels, almost invariably with pneumatic or solid rubber tires of the same type used on bicycles, and axles with ball bearings. It was designed in the 1890s, one of the last horse-drawn vehicles manufactured, and it included such innovations as tubular steel running gear.

which the vehicle was built varied widely. The coal-box buggy and, especially, the piano-box, or square-box, buggy enjoyed great popularity. Without a top a buggy was usually called a runabout, or a driving wagon, and if it had a standing top it was called a Jenny Lind.

The buggy became the universal American vehicle, and by the 1870s its popularity, along with that of the road cart and the spring wagon, brought about the mass production of carriages in Cincinnati, Ohio, and other carriage-building centres. This led to price reductions that further stimulated the popularity of the buggy. It was the Model T Ford of its day, and it continued to be widely used for 10 or 15 years into the 20th century.

CHAPTER 2

History of the Automobile

Unlike many other major inventions, the original idea of the automobile cannot be attributed to a single individual. The idea certainly occurred long before it was first recorded in the *Iliad*, in which Homer (in Alexander Pope's translation) states that Vulcan in a single day made 20 tricycles, which:

> *Wondrous to tell instinct with spirit roll'ed*
> *From place to place, around the blest abodes,*
> *Self-moved, obedient to the beck of gods.*

Leonardo da Vinci considered the idea of a self-propelled vehicle in the 15th century. In 1760 a Swiss clergyman, J.H. Genevois, suggested mounting small windmills on a cartlike vehicle, their power to be used to wind springs that would move the road wheel. Genevois's idea probably derived from a windmill cart of about 1714. Two-masted wind carriages were running in the Netherlands in 1600, and a speed of 30 km (20 miles) per hour with a load of 28 passengers was claimed for at least one of them. The first recorded suggestion of wind use was probably Robert Valturio's unrealized plan (1472) for a cart powered by windmills geared to the wheels.

Other inventors considered the possibilities of clockwork. Sometime around 1748 a carriage propelled by a large clockwork engine was demonstrated in Paris by the versatile inventor Jacques de Vaucanson.

The air engine is thought to have originated with a 17th-century German physicist, Otto von Guericke. Guericke invented an air pump and was probably the first to make metal pistons, cylinders, and connecting rods, the basic components of the reciprocating engine. In the 17th century a Dutch inventor, Christiaan Huygens, produced an engine that worked by air pressure developed by explosion of a powder charge. Denis Papin of France built a model engine on the vacuum principle, using the condensation of steam to produce the vacuum. An air engine was patented in England in 1799, and a grid of compressor stations was proposed to service vehicles. An air-powered vehicle is said to have been produced in 1832.

Steam propulsion was proposed as early as the 16th century. In 1678 Ferdinand Verbiest, a Belgian Jesuit missionary to China, made a model steam carriage based on a principle suggestive of the modern turbine.

In the 18th century a French scientist, Philippe Lebon, patented a coal-gas engine and made the first suggestion of electrical ignition. In Paris, Isaac de Rivas made a gas-powered vehicle in 1807; his engine used hydrogen gas as fuel, the valves and ignition were operated by hand, and the timing problem appears to have been difficult.

THE AGE OF STEAM

Most historians agree that Nicolas-Joseph Cugnot of France was the constructor of the first true automobile. Cugnot's vehicle was a huge, heavy, steam-powered tricycle. His 1769 model was said to have run for 20 minutes at 3.6 km (2.25 miles) per hour while carrying four people, and to have recuperated sufficient steam power to move again after standing for 20 minutes. Cugnot was an artillery officer, and the more or less steam-tight pistons of his engine were made possible by the invention of a drill that accurately machined cannon bores. A replica of Cugnot's second vehicle, partially original, is preserved in the Conservatoire National des Arts et Métiers in Paris.

Cugnot's successors were soon at work, notably in England, although the first post-Cugnot steam carriage appears to have been built in Amiens, France, in 1790. Steam buses were running in Paris about 1800. Oliver Evans of Philadelphia ran an amphibious steam dredge through the streets of that city in 1805. Less well-known were Nathan Read of Salem, Mass., and Apollos Kinsley of Hartford, Conn., both of whom ran steam vehicles during the period 1790–1800. In March 1863 the magazine *Scientific American* described tests of a vehicle that weighed only about 300 kg (650 pounds) and achieved a speed of 30 km (20 miles) per hour. Another American, Frank Curtis of Newburyport, Mass., is remembered for building a personal steam carriage to the order of a Boston man who failed to meet the payment schedule, whereupon Curtis made the first recorded repossession of a motor vehicle.

English inventors were active, and by the 1830s the manufacture and use of steam road carriages was flourishing. James Watt's foreman, William Murdock, ran a model steam carriage on the roads of Cornwall in 1784, and Robert Fourness showed a working three-cylinder tractor in 1788. Watt was opposed to the use of steam engines for such purposes; his low-pressure steam engine would have been too bulky for road use in any case, and all the British efforts in steam derived from the earlier researches of Thomas Savery and Thomas Newcomen.

Richard Trevithick developed Murdock's ideas, and at least one of his carriages, with driving wheels 3 metres (10 feet) in diameter, ran in London. Sir Goldsworthy Gurney, the first commercially successful steam carriage builder, based his design upon an unusually efficient boiler. He was not, however, convinced that smooth wheels could grip a roadway, and so he arranged propulsion on his first vehicle by iron legs digging into the road surface. His second vehicle weighed only 1,360 kg (3,000 pounds) and was said to be capable of carrying six persons. He made trips as long as 135 km (84 miles) in a running time of 9 hours and 30 minutes and once recorded a speed of 27 km (17 miles) per hour.

Gurney equipment was used on the Gloucester-Cheltenham service of four daily round trips; under favourable conditions the equipment could complete the 15 km (9 miles) in 45 minutes. Between Feb. 27 and June 22, 1831, steam coaches ran 6,400 km (4,000 miles) on this route, carrying some 3,000 passengers. The equipment was noisy, smoky, destructive of roadways, and admittedly dangerous; hostility arose, and it was common for drivers to find the way blocked with heaps of stones or felled trees. Nevertheless, numerous passengers had been carried by steam carriage before the railways had accepted their first paying passenger.

The most successful era of the steam coaches in Britain was the 1830s. Ambitious routes were run, including one from London to Cambridge. But by 1840 it was clear that the steam carriages had little future. They had had much to contend with, including the anti-machinery attitude of the public and the enmity of the horse-coach interests, which resulted in such penalties as a charge of £5 for passing a tollgate that cost a horse coach only three pence. The crushing blow was the Locomotives on Highways Act of 1865, which reduced permissible speeds on public roads to 3 km (2 miles) per hour within cities and 6 km (4 miles) per hour in rural areas. This legislation was known as the Red Flag Act because of its requirement that every steam carriage mount a crew of three, one to precede it carrying a red flag of warning. The act was amended in 1878, but it was not repealed until 1896, by which time its provisions had effectively stifled the development of road transport in the British Isles.

The decline of the steam carriage did not prevent continued effort in the field, and much attention was given to the steam tractor for use as a prime mover. Beginning about 1868, Britain was the scene of a vogue for light steam-powered personal carriages; if the popularity of these vehicles had not been legally hindered, it would certainly have resulted in widespread enthusiasm for motoring in the 1860s rather than in the 1890s. Some of the steamers could carry as few as two people and were capable of speeds of 32 km (20 miles) per hour. The public climate remained unfriendly, however.

Light steam cars were being built in the United States, France, Germany, and Denmark during the same period, and it is possible to argue that the line from Cugnot's lumbering vehicle runs unbroken to the 20th-century steam automobiles made as late as 1926. The grip of the steam automobile on the American imagination has been strong ever since the era of the Stanley brothers—one of whose "steamers" took the world speed record at 205.45 km (127.66 miles) per hour in 1906. The car designed by them and sold as the Locomobile became the first commercially successful American-made automobile (about 1,000 were built in 1900). It is estimated that there are still hundreds of steam cars in the United States, most of them in running order.

EARLY ELECTRIC AUTOMOBILES

At the beginning of the 20th century, 40 percent of American automobiles were powered by steam, 38 percent by electricity, and 22 percent by gasoline. In the face of the gasoline car's unreliability, noise, and vibration and the steamer's complications and thirst, the electric offered attractive selling points: notably, instant self-start, silent operation, and minimal maintenance. The first automobile to exceed 100 km (60 miles) per hour was an electric (Camille Jenatzy's *La Jamais Contente*, 1899). An electric, also Jenatzy's, had been the easy winner in 1898 of a French hill-climb contest to assay the three forms of power.

Invention of the storage battery by Gaston Planté of France in 1859–60 and its improvement by Camille Faure in 1881 made the electric vehicle possible, and what was probably the first, a tricycle, ran in Paris in 1881. It was followed by other three-wheelers in London (1882) and Boston (1888). The first American battery-powered automobile, built in Des Moines, Iowa, *c.* 1890, by William Morrison, could maintain a speed of 23 km (14 miles) per hour.

The popularity of the electric car was hampered by a lack of battery-charging infrastructure. Prior to 1910, few private homes, even in cities, were wired with electricity, and community charging stations and battery exchange schemes failed to catch on. By 1912 the problem had been overcome, and the electric had its heyday. Some 20 companies were in the trade and 33,842 electric cars were registered in the United States, the country in which they had maximum acceptance. It was another application of battery power, the electric self-starter, that did as much as anything to doom the electric car by eliminating the dreaded hand crank and making the internal-combustion engine car amenable to operation by women. Further, the electric had never really been suited to other than limited urban use because of its low speed (24–32 km [15–20 miles] per hour), short range (50–65 km [30–40 miles]), and lengthy time required for recharging. The heyday of the electric car in America had ended by 1920, although a few manufacturers offered them on special order until World War II. The war, however, gave rise to experiments with small electric cars in fuel-starved France and resulted in extensive use of electric vehicles for milk delivery in Britain, which continued in urban areas there for the rest of the century.

DEVELOPMENT OF THE GASOLINE CAR

Most authorities are inclined to honour Karl Benz and Gottlieb Daimler of Germany as the most important pioneer contributors to the gasoline-engine automobile. Benz ran his first car in 1885, Daimler in 1886. Although there is no reason to believe that Benz had ever seen a motor vehicle before he made his own, he and Daimler had been preceded by Étienne Lenoir in France and Siegfried Marcus in Austria, in 1862 and 1864–65, respectively, but neither Lenoir nor Marcus had persisted. Benz and Daimler did persist—indeed, to such purpose that the successor firm of Daimler AG can trace its origins as far back as 1885 and claim, with PSA Peugeot Citroën SA of France, to be one of the oldest automobile-manufacturing firms in the world. Oddly, Benz and Daimler never met.

The four-stroke principle upon which most modern automobile engines work was discovered by the French engineer Alphonse Beau de Rochas, in 1862, a year before Lenoir ran his car from Paris to Joinville-le-Pont. The four-stroke cycle is often called the Otto cycle, after the German Nikolaus August Otto, who designed an engine on that principle in 1876. De Rochas held prior patents, however, and litigation in the French courts upheld him. Lenoir's engine omitted the compression stroke of the Otto cycle; fuel was drawn into the cylinder on the intake stroke and fired by a spark halfway on the next reciprocal stroke.

The idea for Marcus's 1864–65 car apparently came to him by chance while he was considering the production of illumination by igniting a mixture of gasoline and air with a stream of sparks. The reaction was so violent that it occurred to him to use it as a power source. His first vehicle was a handcart marrying a two-cycle engine geared to the rear wheels without any intervening clutch. It was started by having a strong man lift the rear end while the wheels were spun, after which it ran for a distance of about 180 metres (about 600 feet). Marcus's second model, the 1888–89 car, was sturdy and sufficiently well-preserved to make a demonstration run in the streets of Vienna in 1950, and again in 1987, at a rate of almost 5 km (3 miles) per hour. In 1898 the Austrian Automobile Club arranged an exhibition of motorcars, and Marcus was a guest of honour. Ironically, he denied interest in the idea of the automobile, calling it "a senseless waste of time and effort."

KARL BENZ

Karl Benz was completely dedicated to the proposition that the internal-combustion engine would supersede the horse and revolutionize the world's transportation. He persisted in his efforts to build a gasoline-fueled vehicle in the face of many obstacles, including lack of money to the point of poverty and the bitter objections of his associates, who considered him unbalanced on the subject.

Benz ran his first car, a three-wheeler powered by a two-cycle, one-cylinder engine, on a happy and triumphant day early in 1885. He circled a cinder track beside his small factory, his workmen running beside the car, his wife running too, clapping her hands. The little machine made four circuits of the track, stalling only twice before a broken chain stopped it. Even Max Rose, Benz's skeptical partner, whose money had made the car possible, conceded that he was mildly impressed. Yet like Siegfried Marcus, Rose remained convinced to the end of his association with Benz that there was no future in the horseless carriage.

Benz made his first sale to a Parisian named Émile Roger in 1888. Gradually, the soundness of his design and the quality and care that went into the material and the construction of his cars bore weight, and they sold well. That year he employed some 50 workmen to build the tricycle car; in 1893 he began to make a four-wheeler.

In his way, Benz was almost as dogmatic and reactionary as Marcus had been. He objected to redesign of his original cars, and some authorities believe that he was never really convinced that his original concepts had been improved upon.

GOTTLIEB DAIMLER

Gunsmithing was Gottlieb Daimler's first vocation, and he showed marked talent, but he abandoned the trade to go to engineering school, studying in Germany, England, and France. In Germany he worked for various engineering and machining concerns, including the Karlsruhe Maschinenbaugesellschaft, a firm that much earlier had employed Benz.

In 1872 Daimler became technical director of Otto's firm, then building stationary gasoline engines. During the next decade, important work was done on the four-stroke engine. Daimler brought in several brilliant researchers, among them Wilhelm Maybach, but in 1882 both Daimler and Maybach resigned because of Daimler's conviction that Otto did not understand the potential of the internal-combustion engine. They set up a shop in Bad Cannstatt and built an air-cooled, one-cylinder engine. The first high-speed internal-combustion engine, it was designed to run at

900 revolutions per minute (rpm). For comparison, Benz's first tricycle engine had operated at only 250 rpm.

Daimler and Maybach built a second engine and mounted it on a wooden bicycle fitted with an outrigger, which first ran on Nov. 10, 1885. The next year the first Daimler four-wheeled road vehicle was made—a carriage modified to be driven by a one-cylinder engine. Daimler appears to have believed that the first phase of the automobile era would be a mass conversion of carriages to engine drive; Benz apparently thought of the motorcar as a separate device. Daimler's licensees in France were René Panhard and Émile Levassor. In 1889 they entered the field independently, and the Panhard-Levassor designs of 1891–94 are of primary importance. They were true automobiles, not carriages modified for self-propulsion.

Daimler's 1889 car was a departure from previous practice. It was based on a framework of light tubing, it had the engine in the rear, its wheels were driven by a belt, and it was steered by a tiller. Remarkably, it had four speeds. This car had obvious commercial value, and in the following year the Daimler Motoren-Gesellschaft was founded. The British Daimler automobile was started as a manufactory licensed by the German company but later became quite independent of it. (To distinguish machines made by the two firms in the early years, the German cars are usually referred to as Cannstatt-Daimlers.) The Daimler and Benz firms were merged in 1926, and products thereafter have been sold under the name Mercedes-Benz.

OTHER EUROPEAN DEVELOPMENTS

In France the giants were De Dion-Bouton, Peugeot SA (now PSA Peugeot Citroën SA), and Renault (which still exists). The Italians were later in the field: the

Stefanini-Martina of 1896 is thought of as the foundation of the industry in Italy, and Isotta-Fraschini was founded about 1898. Giovanni Agnelli founded Fiat SpA in 1899, saw it grow into one of the weightiest industrial complexes in the world, and maintained personal control until his death in 1945. Fabricators of lesser puissance but great repute were Lancia, Alfa Romeo SpA, Maserati, and Ferrari (all now part of Fiat), for years the standard against which other Grand Prix and Gran Turismo motorcars were judged.

The smaller European countries produced makes that were to remain less well-known: the Belgian Minerva, Métallurgique, and Excelsior; the Swiss Martini; the Austrian Austro-Daimler, Steyr, and Gräf und Stift; and the Czechoslovakian Skoda and Tatra, the latter technically interesting for its big rear-mounted V-8 engine. Spain had the Elizalde, and the classic Hispano-Suiza by the great Swiss designer Marc Birkigt was Spanish-financed. The oldest automobile still in running order at the beginning of the 21st century was thought to be an 1884 De Dion-Bouton.

THE UNITED STATES

The Daimler and Benz claims to the invention of the automobile were attacked in 1895 when U.S. patent 549,160 was granted to George B. Selden as inventor of the automobile. Selden had filed his application on May 8, 1879, although he had not at that time built an automobile. He was successful in an effort to keep the patent pending for 16 years.

Most authorities credit Charles E. Duryea and J. Frank Duryea with creating the first successful American gasoline-powered automobile, in 1892–93. The concept of the car apparently originated with Charles, and the machine was built by Frank. The Duryea consisted of

The first National Auto Show, held at Madison Square Garden in New York City, 1900. Encyclopædia Britannica, Inc.

a one-cylinder gasoline engine, with electrical ignition, installed in a secondhand carriage. It first ran on Sept. 21, 1893. Driving a later model, J. Frank Duryea won the first automobile race in America in which more than two cars competed, the Chicago Times-Herald Race from Chicago to Evanston, Ill., and return, in November 1895; the distance was 87.48 km (54.36 miles). The Duryea Motor Wagon Company built 13 cars in 1896, and variations on cars built by the brothers, who soon separated, remained on the market until 1917.

The Duryea was certainly not the first American-built road vehicle. A number of steam carriages had been built after Oliver Evans's first example. Nor was the Duryea the first American internal-combustion automobile. Sephaniah Reese, a machinist in Plymouth, Pa., built a graceful gasoline-powered tricycle believed by historians to have been completed in 1887. Henry Nadig, another Pennsylvania inventor, completed a vehicle and tested it in 1891, the same year as John William Lambert of Ohio City, Ohio, and Charles Black of Indianapolis, Ind. William T. Harris of Baltimore and Gottfried Schloemer of Milwaukee, Wis., built successful cars in 1892. The Reese, Nadig, Black, and Schloemer cars still exist. Elwood Haynes followed the Duryea brothers with a gasoline car demonstrated in Kokomo, Ind., on July 4, 1894. Charles

James Ward Packard, the inventive engineer who founded the Packard Motor Company, is shown here in one of the company's first custom models. It was still a one-cylinder car; the crank can be seen at the side. These 1902 Packards were the first to have wood artillery wheels and were beginning to boast something fancy in the way of fenders. Headlights were considered an accessory and cost the purchaser extra. Encyclopædia Britannica, Inc.

Brady King built a car in Detroit, the first of the millions to issue from the city, that first ran on March 6, 1896.

Ransom Eli Olds, whose name is familiar from the long-lived Oldsmobile, was also active in gasoline-engine research in the 1890s, after initially being interested in steam; so were Alexander Winton and James Ward Packard. By 1898 more than 100 companies had been organized with the intent of automobile manufacture.

The three-horsepower, curved-dash Oldsmobile surpassed the steam Locomobile as America's best-selling car in 1902, when 2,750 of them were sold. The company's prosperity was noted by others, and, from 1904 to 1908, 241 automobile-manufacturing firms went into business in the United States. One of these was the Ford Motor Company, which was organized as a corporation in June 1903 and sold its first car the following month. The company produced 1,700 cars during its first full year of business.

FORD AND THE AUTOMOTIVE REVOLUTION

Henry Ford produced eight versions of cars before the Model T of 1908, with which his name became synonymous; these were the models A, B, C, F, K, N, R, and S. They were not remarkable automobiles, but public response to the less expensive ones (the firm made some fairly costly cars at first) indicated the soundness of Ford's idea—to turn the automobile from a luxury and a plaything into a necessity by making it cheap, versatile, and easy to maintain.

By the mid-1920s the American automobile had won the revolution Ford had begun. The country was on wheels, and the manufacture and sale of automobiles had become an important component in the American economy. The

MODEL T

Conceived by Henry Ford as practical, affordable transportation for the common man, the Model T automobile quickly became prized for its low cost, durability, versatility, and ease of maintenance. More than 15 million Model Ts were built in Detroit and Highland Park, Mich., by the Ford Motor Company from 1908 until 1927. (The automobile was also assembled at a Ford plant in Manchester, Eng., and at plants in continental Europe.) Assembly-line production allowed the price of the touring car version to be lowered from $850 in 1908 to less than $300 in 1925. At such prices the Model T at times comprised as much as 40 percent of all cars sold in the United States. Even before it lost favour to larger, more powerful, and more luxurious cars, the Model T, known popularly as the "Tin Lizzie" or the "flivver," had become an American folkloric symbol, essentially realizing Ford's goal to "democratize the automobile."

The Model T was offered in several body styles, including a five-seat touring car, a two-seat runabout, and a seven-seat town car. All bodies were mounted on a uniform 100-inch-wheelbase chassis. A choice of colours was originally available, but from 1913 to 1925 the car was mass-produced in only one colour—black. The engine was simple and efficient, with all four cylinders cast in a single block and the cylinder head detachable for easy access and repair. The engine generated 20 horsepower and propelled the car to modest top speeds of 65–70 km (40–45 miles) per hour. In most models the engine was started by a hand crank, which activated a magneto connected to the flywheel, but after 1920 some models were equipped with battery-powered starters. The transmission, consisting of two forward gears and one reverse, was of the planetary type, controlled by foot pedals rather than the more common hand lever used in sliding-gear transmissions. Spark and throttle were controlled by a hand lever on the steering column. The 10-gallon fuel tank was located under the front seat. Because gasoline was fed to the engine only by gravity, and also because the reverse gear offered more power than the forward gears, the Model T frequently had to be driven up a steep hill backward. Such deficiencies, along with its homely appearance, less-than-comfortable ride at top speeds, and incessant rattling, made the Model T the butt of much affectionate humour in innumerable jokes, songs, poems, and stories.

closed car was no longer exclusively a rich man's possession. In 1920 most cars had been open models, the occupants protected from the weather by canvas-and-isinglass side curtains. The Essex coach, a no-frills two-door sedan introduced in 1922 by the Hudson Motor Car Company, reduced the cost of sheltered motoring to that of a touring car. Ten years later, Detroit manufacturers were producing closed models almost exclusively.

The 1920s saw the emergence of the great European producers—Austin, Morris, and Singer in England, Fiat in Italy, and Citroën in France. Universal motor transportation was a long way off, but the concept of the small car

Ford Motor Company plant, River Rouge, west of Detroit, Mich., c. 1930s. Built between 1917 and 1925, it became the model for assembly-line production, turning parts at one end into finished cars at the other. Encyclopædia Britannica, Inc.

that found expression in the Austin Seven and the Fiat Topolino, two of the descendants of Ettore Bugatti's tiny Bébé Peugeot of 1911, was to have a profound effect.

By the middle of the decade, the American industry had become international. Ford had been assembling Model Ts in Britain since 1911, and General Motors Corporation bought the British Vauxhall and German Opel companies. Chrysler and Hudson, too, began assembly in Europe and other parts of the globe. The American car had established a good export trade after World War I, by which time it was recognized as robust, reliable, and cheap—so much so that several countries adopted taxation and

Cars being assembled on the main assembly line at the Ford Motor Company factory at Dagenham, Essex, Eng., which was the largest automobile-assembly plant in Europe at its opening in 1931. Encyclopædia Britannica, Inc.

duties against it. By the beginning of the 1930s, these policies disadvantaged the large car in Europe such that a new genre of small cars, little larger than the Austin Seven, was created for that market. The standard Ford was no longer a world car.

A significant stream of technological advancements characterized the 1920s and '30s. In addition to four-wheel brakes, almost exclusively hydraulic by 1936, and independent front suspensions, heaters and radios became popular accessories, and transmissions with synchronized gears made driving easier. As the six-cylinder engine had largely replaced the four by 1916, so the "straight eight" was adopted by most manufacturers by 1930. An important exception was Ford's famous V-8 of 1932, notable for its single casting and lively performance.

THE AGE OF THE CLASSIC CARS

The decade 1925–35 was notable not only for the appearance of many new small automobiles but also for the building of many ultra-large ones. The years from 1925 to 1948 are cited by collectors of automobiles as the "classic years," a period that saw the rise of the luxurious fast motorcar to a peak it seems unlikely to reach again. The first name in this field was Rolls-Royce Ltd., founded in 1906. Most Rolls-Royce chassis are designed for limousine and large sedan bodies, but the firm once made a comparatively light car (called the Twenty), and it has throughout its history produced fast models in addition to its regular line—e.g., after World War II, the Continental, built under the Bentley Motors Ltd. label.

Other classic motorcars included the Hispano-Suiza of Spain and France; the Bugatti, Delage, Delahaye, Hotchkiss, Talbot (Darracq), and Voisin of France; the

Duesenberg, Cadillac, Packard, and Pierce-Arrow of the United States; the Horch, Maybach, and Mercedes-Benz of Germany; the Belgian Minerva; and the Italian Isotta-Fraschini. These were costly machines, priced roughly from $7,500 to $40,000, fast (145 to 210 km [90 to 130 miles] per hour), as comfortable as the state of the art would allow, and limited in luxury only by the purse of the purchaser. The great custom coach builders of England who furnished bodies for Rolls-Royce machines, unruffled by the whims of their clients, were prepared to satisfy any request, whether for upholstery in matched ostrich hide with ivory buttons or for a dashboard in rosewood.

The most expensive standard automobile of which there exist convincing records was the Type 41 Bugatti, produced in the 1920s by Ettore Bugatti, an Italian of extraordinary gifts who built cars in France, most of them racing and sports types, from 1909 to 1939. The Type 41 Bugatti, also called La Royale, was cataloged at a chassis price of 500,000 francs, then about $20,000. Only six of the cars were built.

The stock market collapse of 1929 signaled the twilight of the really luxurious motorcar. After World War II even Rolls-Royce abandoned its policy of producing a standard chassis for custom-made bodies and offered a standard sedan that could be bought straight off the showroom floor.

With the demise of the luxury car market came also a great downsizing of the industry. The Great Depression in America, and its fallout in other countries, resulted in the failure of most independent manufacturers and caused others to market lower-priced cars. As a result, the auto market in the United States became dominated by the "Big Three"—General Motors, Ford, and Chrysler—and similar effects were felt overseas.

EUROPEAN POSTWAR DESIGNS

When automobile manufacture was resumed in 1946 after a lull during World War II, the effect of Italian ideas on the world's automobile body designers was profound. Pininfarina of Turin was the best-known of the coach builders who established the characteristic Italian approach: grace, lightness in line and substance, and minimal use of decoration. Designs clearly derivative of those of Italian origin appeared everywhere, and manufacturers in France, the United Kingdom, and the United States contracted for the services of Italian *carrozzerie* (body factories).

The worldwide appeal of the American car had faded. Not only were the cars too large and expensive to operate in lands recovering from war, but those countries were in dire need of cash from export trade. For the first time since early in the century, the United States began importing cars in significant numbers. A factor in this was the return from duty in Europe of servicemen who had previously never seen the sheer variety of automobiles the world afforded. The sports car, designed for pleasure, was particularly new to young Americans. The characteristics of automobiles such as the British two-seater MG, plus their availability at a time of short domestic supply, made them attractive, and the importation of European-made models into the United States increased rapidly. At first, most of these were British, but by the mid-1950s the Volkswagen, originally envisioned by Adolf Hitler as a "people's car" for Germany, had a firm grip on the American market, accounting for half the import sales.

In engineering, much American experimentation followed research begun by the European automotive industry: development of gas turbine engines, fuel-injection systems, disc brakes, rear-engine and later, conversely, front-wheel-drive models. The turbines did not fulfill their promise, but the other advances eventually became common practice.

Front-wheel-drive had largely been abandoned after the 1930s, although the French had great success with the "Traction Avant" Citroën. Swedish aircraft manufacturer Saab AB used it too, for its entry into the automobile market in 1950. It was the British Mini, designed by Sir Alec Issigonis and sold under both Austin and Morris names, that pioneered the front-drive concept as it is now known. Issigonis was attempting to gain the greatest space efficiency in a small car. In order to achieve this he pushed the wheels out to the far corners of the envelope, and to get maximum passenger room inside he turned the engine sideways and located it directly atop the transmission. The Mini was spectacularly successful, although it was a dozen years before the concept was taken up by others, such as the Japanese with the Honda Civic.

V-8s and Chrome in America

In the United States, automobile racing in the years around 1910 was drawing the biggest crowds in American sports history. It began to regain popularity following World War II. By the mid-1950s motor racing had again become a high-ranking American spectator sport, and by 1969 estimated attendance was 41,300,000, higher than that for baseball or football. Only horse racing showed a total higher than auto racing. In the 1950s and '60s American manufacturers returned to testing new engineering designs at automobile races (a standard practice in 1900–30). Ford was most successful, winning the Le Mans 24-hour Grand Prix race—the first American-built car to do so—in 1966 and 1967 and producing, in a remarkably short time, a racing engine that dominated major American tracks.

The public now craved performance, and the V-8 engine, increasingly with high compression and overhead valves, became near-universal in the United States. More and more cars were delivered with automatic transmissions, first used by Oldsmobile in 1940, which made it unnecessary for the driver to shift gears. Air conditioning, an unsatisfactory experiment before World War II, was again offered, and the introduction of a compact system by Pontiac in 1954, capable of installation completely in the engine compartment, resulted in greatly increasing popularity.

From the 1930s onward, cars had become more streamlined. Fenders became part of the body, as opposed to appendages on it. To provide contrast on otherwise undistinguished shapes, designers began applying bright, chromium-plated trim and adopted multi-toned colour schemes. By 1956 most cars could be ordered in three different hues, and three years later the Cadillac, which in 1948 had pioneered fenders fashioned after the tail fins of airplanes, boasted taillights nearly four feet off the ground.

AMERICAN COMPACT CARS

While the size of the standard American motorcar increased steadily from the late 1940s to the early 1960s, a small segment of the population was demonstrating a preference for smaller cars and for comparatively uncluttered styling. The success of the Volkswagen and other small cars, bolstered by the 1958 recession, eventually led the major American producers simultaneously to undertake the production of automobiles generically termed "compact." With wheelbases of 269 to 279 centimetres (106 to 110 inches), the Ford Falcon, Chrysler Valiant, and Chevrolet Corvair were smaller than most American cars but still larger than the average European models. By the mid-1960s a demand for more highly individualized luxury models of compact size had brought lines of "intermediate" cars from all manufacturers. The Ford Mustang, basically a Falcon modified into a sporty coupe, set the pace for a new genre of what came to be known as "pony cars." A similar exercise in "market engineering" at General Motors created the "muscle car," an intermediate-size car with a large engine from the top of the line, as typified by the Pontiac GTO.

JAPANESE CARS

Although Datsun (Nissan Motor Company, Ltd.) had been making cars since 1914, the majority of automobile production in Japan before 1936 came from a subsidiary of Ford in Yokohama. As a result of laws requiring local ownership, however, Datsun and Toyota Motor Corporation, the latter originally a textile machinery company, dominated from that time. Post-World War II recovery was slow, a mere 13,000 cars produced in 1955, but both firms began exporting to the United States in 1958. The first such car to sell in any quantity was the Toyota Corona, introduced in 1967. While $100 more expensive than the Volkswagen Beetle, it was slightly larger, better-appointed, and offered an optional automatic transmission.

The 1970s were stagnant years for American automobile design, as engineering was directed toward meeting safety and environmental regulations resulting from laws enacted by Congress beginning in 1966. Engines were modified to emit fewer pollutants, at first sacrificing efficiency, although fuel shortages and price increases during the decade made this a counterproductive approach. Safety advances included redundant braking systems, seat and shoulder belts, and strengthened bumpers. The availability of fresh designs with high perceived quality from the Japanese manufacturers, however, severely tilted traditional buying patterns. Honda, formerly a motorcycle manufacturer, offered an advanced compound vortex controlled combustion (CVCC) chamber, which easily met American emissions standards at a time when American manufacturers were arguing that it was impossible. Honda's Accord model, introduced in 1976, offered refinement and economy superior to comparable American models, albeit at a slightly higher price. The Accord was an immediate hit and resulted in construction of a Honda manufacturing plant in Ohio, the first of what would be many "transplant" operations. In 1989 the Accord became the best-selling passenger car model in the United States, a position that it held in many subsequent years.

FROM STATION WAGONS TO VANS AND SPORT UTILITY VEHICLES

Until 1948 the station wagon had been a utility vehicle, with a wooden body and little in the way of creature comforts. In 1949 Chrysler introduced an all-steel wagon in its entry-level Plymouth line. Within three years all manufacturers were offering them, and a genre of utilitarian yet stylish family transportation vehicles was born.

By the mid-1980s the station wagon became largely extinct as the front-drive minivan rose in popularity. Essentially Issigonis's Mini packaging applied to a larger box, the minivan featured a transverse power package with the rest of the vehicle devoted to passengers and cargo. The first example was the Dodge Caravan, which was quickly imitated by others and taken up overseas, where it was known as a multipurpose vehicle, or MPV. General Motors introduced a wholly new range of transverse-engine front-drive sedans in 1980, paving the way for this to become the dominant automotive architecture within a decade. These were generally smaller and lighter than their predecessors and were powered by smaller engines. The V-6 engine soon replaced the V-8 as the most popular choice.

The 1990s exhibited another change in customer preferences, as the medium-sized four-wheel-drive vehicle, a descendant of the World War II Jeep, became immensely popular. Generically known as sport-utility vehicles (SUVs), the type eventually reached luxury nameplates like Cadillac and Porsche. Derided by some as a frivolous fashion statement and unwise use of resources, the SUV craze was aided by stable fuel prices in the mid-1980s. At the beginning of the 21st century, most manufacturers were introducing smaller, more carlike "crossovers," a trend that intensified through the first decade of that century as the rising cost of gasoline dampened enthusiasm for full-size SUVs.

ALTERNATIVE-FUEL VEHICLES

The internal-combustion engine dominated the bulk of the 20th century, its success perpetuated by low fuel prices. Businesses helped to entrench gasoline-powered vehicles by establishing the infrastructure—gasoline stations—to support them. However, concerns about climate change, the political stability of oil-producing countries, and the expense of discovering new oil fields have driven research into alternative-fuel vehicles.

DIESEL

After World War II the diesel engine, particularly for light trucks and taxis, became popular in Europe because of its superior fuel economy and various tax incentives. During the 1970s General Motors converted some gasoline passenger-car engines to the more economical compression-ignition diesel operation, and Mercedes-Benz, Volkswagen, and Peugeot marketed diesel lines in America that derived from their European models. The ebbing of fuel shortages and the easing of gasoline prices, combined with various drawbacks to diesel engines (noise, poor cold-weather starting, limited fuel and service in some communities), reduced American demand by the early 1980s. Europe, which had not embraced diesels for private passenger cars, reversed course with the development of environmentally friendly common rail direct-injection diesel engines in the late 1990s. By 2005 diesel cars represented roughly half of all European passenger car sales.

ELECTRIC

The first of the fuel crises, in 1973–74, rekindled interest in electric vehicles in America. Numerous experimenters and entrepreneurs began work on battery electric cars, the most successful being the CitiCar built by a Florida company, Sebring Vanguard, Inc. The CitiCar had a plastic, wedge-shaped, two-seater body over a welded aluminum chassis. Lead-acid batteries supplied power to a 3.5-horsepower General Electric motor. With about 2,600 built between 1974 and 1976 (and another 2,000 of its successor, the ComutaCar, built between 1978 and 1981), the CitiCar was the most prolific of the late-20th-century electrics. Ultimately, the falling price of oil put an end to electric car sales.

Subsequent alternative propulsion programs were driven by environmental concerns. In 1990 the California Air Resources Board mandated that within eight years all auto manufacturers were to ensure that 2 percent of their sales in the state be "zero emission" vehicles. For all practical purposes this meant battery electrics. General

Motors took this edict most seriously, beginning work on an aluminum backbone frame, composite plastic body, and low-rolling-resistance tires. Introduced in 1996 as the General Motors EV1, it was offered on lease through Saturn dealers in Arizona and California. Only 800 were contracted for, and production halted in 2000, with 100 remaining in service through 2005. In 1998–99 General Motors and Ford also offered battery electric pickup trucks, most of which were placed with government fleets. The shortcoming of all these battery electrics was their limited range—less than 100 miles with lead-acid batteries. More capable nickel–metal hydride cells were inordinately expensive. The faltering efforts resulted in relaxation of the California mandate. Despite these setbacks, research and development continued on electric vehicles, with Nissan and Tesla Motors among those manufacturers that subsequently released all-electric vehicles in the United States.

Electric vehicles do have significant difficulties. Given the limitations of current battery capacities and the current technologies that partly recharge batteries by using energy produced while braking, electric vehicles at this time are best suited for stop-and-go, short-range city driving. Before fully electric vehicles can realistically be expected to replace fuel-powered cars, charging and battery-exchange stations will have to be put in place everywhere cars are driven—not just in a few cities.

Also, even assuming the establishment of networks of charging stations, technological problems would have to be addressed. For instance, many plug-in models take hours to recharge, whereas gasoline-powered cars take only minutes to refuel. Stations that are capable of charging car batteries rapidly are possible in theory, but they would have to be designed and operated in such a manner that they would avoid straining municipal power grids.

Also, as long as electric power plants continue to run on fossil fuels such as coal, recharging fleets of plug-in electric cars will not eliminate the emission of carbon into the atmosphere.

ELECTRIC-GASOLINE HYBRIDS

In 1997 Toyota introduced its four-passenger Prius hybrid to the Japanese market. Combining a small gasoline engine and an electric motor through a sophisticated control system, the Prius uses gasoline power only when necessary to supplement electric propulsion or to recharge its batteries. (That same year in Europe, the hybrid Audi Duo was introduced, but its poor sales led European manufacturers to focus on diesel designs.) Honda was the first manufacturer to offer a hybrid in the American market, the two-passenger Insight, in December 1999.

In order to establish hybrid technology in the American marketplace, Toyota initially offered substantial discounts on the Prius when it introduced it to the United States in

2006 Toyota Prius. Toyota Motor Sales, USA.

ELECTRIC AND HYBRID VEHICLES DURING THE GREAT RECESSION

The gathering economic forces of 2008–09 prompted renewed interest not only in hybrids but also in fully electric vehicles and so-called plug-in hybrids (models with an extra capacity to recharge their batteries off the power grid). During his campaign for the U.S. presidency in 2008, Barack Obama promised that half of all vehicles purchased by the federal government by 2012 would be plug-in hybrids or fully electric. In August 2009 Obama, now president, announced that $2.4 billion of his economic stimulus package had been awarded to some 48 automakers or parts manufacturers in order to increase production of electric vehicles. Another $400 million was laid aside to fund projects aimed at developing infrastructure.

Other countries made similar efforts. China's government announced that it would provide subsidies for research and would also subsidize the purchase of electric or hybrid vehicles for use in Chinese taxi fleets and by government agencies. Britain's Prime Minister Gordon Brown said in July 2009 that he wanted all new cars sold in his country by 2020 to be electric or hybrid—though British automakers retorted that Brown's offer earlier in the year to subsidize purchases of electric vehicles would have little effect on sales.

Auto companies scrambled to capitalize on new grants and subsidies. General Motors, which by July 2009 was majority-owned by the U.S. government, rolled out its new electric car, the Chevrolet Volt, in late 2010. The Volt was an "extended range" model, one whose batteries would be recharged overnight by a plug-in connection or on the road by a small gasoline engine. Also in 2009, Nissan Motor Co. announced production of the Leaf, a fully electric automobile that would boast zero tailpipe carbon emissions.

Efforts were being made on the infrastructure end as well. The mayor of London, vowing to make that city the "electric car capital of Europe," announced plans to have as many as 25,000 charging points installed in accessible areas by 2015. In Yokohama, Japan, the U.S.-based company Better Place, founded by Israeli-born entrepreneur Shai Agassi, demonstrated the prototype of an automated battery-exchange station that it intended to install throughout Israel and Denmark as part of a program to encourage a mass market for electric automobiles.

2000. The U.S. and some state governments also offered tax incentives and other perquisites (such as unlimited use of commuter lanes and exemption from paying parking meters) to encourage production and sales of alternative-fuel vehicles. Although the Prius offered only a relatively modest increase in fuel economy, the removal of any need to plug the batteries in for recharging overcame the chief drawback to pure electric vehicles.

The Prius was an immediate hit with trend-conscious Californians, with many celebrities choosing to drive hybrids instead of luxury cars, and prospective buyers often had to wait months for delivery. In 2004 the Ford Escape Hybrid (SUV) became the first American hybrid, beating two General Motors trucks, the Chevrolet Silverado and the GMC Sierra, to market by one year. The first luxury hybrid vehicle, the Lexus RX 400h, was released in 2005. In 2010, General Motors introduced the Chevrolet Volt, a car that could drive up to about 35 miles on electric batteries and would then drive using gasoline after the battery was exhausted.

ETHANOL AND FUEL CELLS

In 1999 Brazil mandated that by 2003 all new cars sold in the country had to be FlexFuel vehicles (FFVs)—vehicles certified to run on gasoline containing up to 85 percent ethanol (ethyl alcohol), marketed as E85. This initiative led numerous American, European, and Japanese manufacturers to certify some of their models as E85-compliant, which is indicated by the eighth character in the vehicle identification number, or VIN.

General Motors, Ford, and Chrysler have researched fuel-cell development, assisted by U.S. government grants. However, usable technology for the general public is still years away.

CHAPTER 3

AUTOMOTIVE DESIGN

Passenger cars have emerged as the primary means of family transportation, with an estimated three-quarters of a billion in operation worldwide. One-quarter of these are in the United States, where almost five trillion kilometres (some three trillion miles) are traveled each year. In recent years, Americans have been offered hundreds of different models, about half of them from foreign manufacturers. To capitalize on their proprietary technological advances, manufacturers introduce new designs ever more frequently. With more than 50 million new units built each year worldwide, manufacturers have been able to split the market into many very small segments that nonetheless remain profitable.

New technical developments are recognized to be the key to successful competition. Research and development engineers and scientists have been employed by all automobile manufacturers and suppliers to improve the body, chassis, engine, drivetrain, control systems, safety systems, and emission-control systems.

These outstanding technical advancements are not made without economic consequences. According to a study by Ward's Communications Incorporated, the average cost for a new American car increased $4,700 (in terms of the value of the dollar in 2000) between 1980 and 2001 because of mandated safety and emission-control performance requirements (such as the addition of air bags and catalytic converters). New requirements continued to be implemented in subsequent years. Such increases are in

A Sunday drive in the family Packard, southern Vermont, 1906. Library of Congress, Washington, D.C.

addition to the consumer costs associated with engineering improvements in fuel economy, which may be offset by reduced fuel purchases.

Vehicle design depends to a large extent on its intended use. Automobiles for off-road use must be durable, simple systems with high resistance to severe overloads and extremes in operating conditions. Conversely, products that are intended for high-speed, limited-access road systems require more passenger comfort options, increased engine performance, and optimized high-speed handling and vehicle stability. Stability depends principally on the distribution of weight between the front and rear wheels, the height of the centre of gravity and its position relative to the aerodynamic centre of pressure of the vehicle, suspension characteristics, and the selection of which wheels are used for propulsion. Weight distribution depends principally on the location and size of the engine. The common practice of front-mounted engines exploits the stability that is more readily achieved with this layout. The development of aluminum engines and new manufacturing processes has, however, made it possible to locate the engine at the rear without necessarily compromising stability.

AUTOMOTIVE SYSTEMS AND SUBSYSTEMS

The modern automobile is a complex technical system employing subsystems with specific design functions.

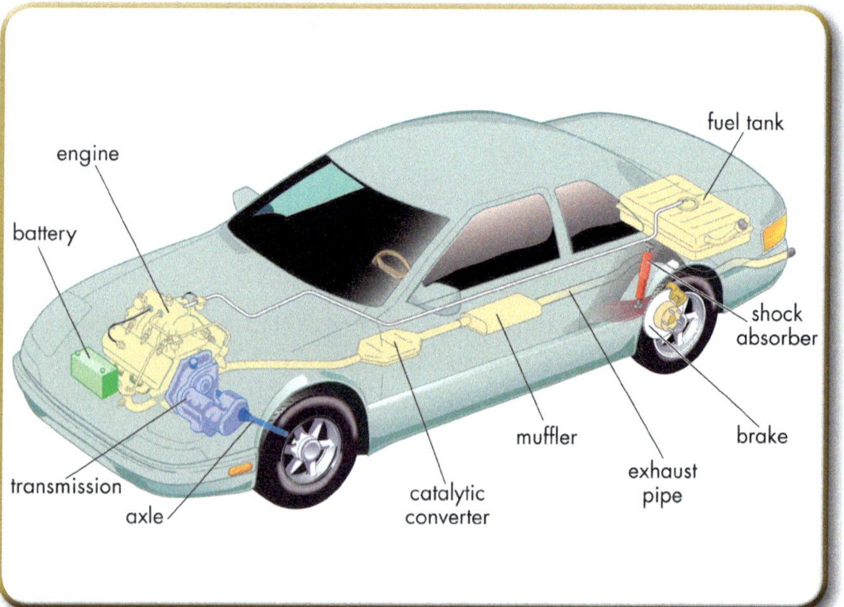

The major functional components of an automobile. Encyclopædia Britannica, Inc.

Some of these consist of thousands of component parts that have evolved from breakthroughs in existing technology or from new technologies such as electronic computers, high-strength plastics, and new alloys of steel and nonferrous metals. Some subsystems have come about as a result of factors such as air pollution, safety legislation, and foreign competition.

BODY

Automotive body designs are frequently categorized according to the number of doors, the arrangement of seats, and the roof structure. Automobile roofs are conventionally supported by pillars on each side of the body. Convertible models with retractable fabric tops rely on the pillar at the side of the windshield for upper body strength, as convertible mechanisms and glass areas are essentially nonstructural. Glass areas have been increased for improved visibility and for aesthetic reasons.

The high cost of new factory tools makes it impractical for manufacturers to produce totally new designs every year. Completely new designs usually have been programmed on three- to six-year cycles with generally minor refinements appearing during the cycle. In the past, as many as four years of planning and new tool purchasing were needed for a completely new design. Computer-aided design (CAD), testing by use of computer simulations, and computer-aided manufacturing (CAM) techniques may now be used to reduce this time requirement by 50 percent or more.

Automotive bodies are generally formed out of sheet steel. The steel is alloyed with various elements to improve its ability to be formed into deeper depressions without wrinkling or tearing in manufacturing presses. Steel is used because of its general availability, low cost, and good workability. For certain applications, however, other materials, such as aluminum, fibreglass, and carbon-fibre reinforced plastic, are used because of their special properties. Polyamide, polyester, polystyrene, polypropylene, and ethylene plastics have been formulated for greater toughness, dent resistance, and resistance to brittle deformation. These materials are used for body panels. Tooling for plastic components generally costs less and requires less time to develop than that for steel components and therefore may be changed by designers at a lower cost.

To protect bodies from corrosive elements and to maintain their strength and appearance, special priming and painting processes are used. Bodies are first dipped in cleaning baths to remove oil and other foreign matter. They then go through a succession of dip and spray cycles. Enamel and acrylic lacquer are both in common use. Electrodeposition of the sprayed paint, a process in which the paint spray is given an electrostatic charge and then attracted to the surface by a high voltage, helps assure that an even coat is applied and that hard-to-reach areas are covered. Ovens with conveyor lines are used to speed the drying process in the factory. Galvanized steel with a protective zinc coating and corrosion-resistant stainless steel are used in body areas that are more likely to corrode.

CHASSIS

In most passenger cars through the middle of the 20th century a pressed-steel frame—the vehicle's chassis—formed a skeleton on which the engine, wheels, axle assemblies, transmission, steering mechanism, brakes, and suspension members were mounted. The body was flexibly bolted to the chassis during a manufacturing process typically referred to as body-on-frame construction. This process is used today for heavy-duty vehicles, such as trucks, which benefit from having a strong central frame subjected to the forces involved in such activities as carrying freight, including the absorption of the movements of the engine and axle that is allowed by the combination of body and frame.

In modern passenger-car designs the chassis frame and the body are combined into a single structural element. In this arrangement, called unit-body (or unibody) construction, the steel body shell is reinforced with braces that make it rigid enough to resist the forces that are applied to it. Separate frames or partial "stub" frames have been used for some cars to achieve better noise-isolation characteristics. The heavier-gauge steel present in modern component designs also tends to absorb energy during impacts and limit intrusion in accidents.

ENGINE

A wide range of engines has been used experimentally and in automotive production. The most successful for automobiles has been the gasoline-fueled reciprocating-piston internal-combustion engine, operating on a four-stroke cycle: intake, compression, combustion (power), and exhaust. As the piston moves during each stroke, it turns the crankshaft. Diesel engines, which are widely used for trucks and buses, involve a single intake valve, fuel-injection nozzle, and exhaust valve. Injected fuel is ignited by its reaction to compressed hot air in the cylinder, a more efficient process than that of the spark-ignition internal-combustion engine.

The gasoline engine was originally selected for automobiles because it could operate more flexibly over a wide range of speeds, and the power developed for a given weight engine was reasonable; it could be produced by economical mass-production methods; and it used a

INTERNAL-COMBUSTION ENGINE

The internal-combustion engine is a device in which the reactants of combustion (oxidizer and fuel) and the products of combustion serve as the working fluids of the engine. Such an engine gains its energy from heat released during the combustion of the nonreacted working fluids, the oxidizer-fuel mixture. This process occurs within the engine and is part of the thermodynamic cycle of the device. Useful work generated by an internal-combustion (IC) engine results from the hot gaseous products of combustion acting on moving surfaces of the engine, such as the face of a piston, a turbine blade, or a nozzle.

Internal-combustion engines are the most broadly applied and widely used power-generating devices currently in existence. Examples include gasoline engines, diesel engines, gas-turbine engines, and rocket-propulsion systems.

Internal-combustion engines are divided into two groups: continuous-combustion engines and intermittent-combustion engines. The continuous-combustion engine is characterized by a steady flow of fuel and oxidizer into the engine. A stable flame is maintained within the engine (e.g., jet engine). The intermittent-combustion engine is characterized by periodic ignition of air and fuel and is commonly referred to as a reciprocating engine. Discrete volumes of air and fuel are processed in a cyclic manner. Gasoline piston engines and diesel engines are examples of this second group.

Internal-combustion engines can be delineated in terms of a series of thermodynamic events. In the continuous-combustion engine, the thermodynamic events occur simultaneously as the oxidizer and fuel and the products of combustion flow steadily through the engine. In the intermittent-combustion engine, by contrast, the events occur in succession and are repeated for each full cycle.

With the exception of rockets (both solid rocket motors and liquid-propellant rocket engines), internal-combustion engines ingest air, then either compress the air and introduce fuel into the air or introduce fuel and compress the air-fuel mixture. Then, common to all internal-combustion engines, the air-fuel mixture is burned, work is extracted from the expansion of the hot gaseous products of combustion, and ultimately the products of combustion are released through the exhaust system. Their operation can be contrasted with that of external-combustion engines (e.g., steam engines), in which the working fluid does not chemically react and energy gain is achieved solely through heat transfer to the working fluid by way of a heat exchanger.

The most common internal-combustion engine is the four-stroke, gasoline-powered, homogeneous-charge, spark-ignition engine. This is because of its outstanding performance as a prime mover in the ground transportation industry. Spark-ignition engines also are used in the aeronautics industry; however, aircraft gas turbines have become the prime movers in this sector because of the emphasis of the aeronautics industry on range, speed, and passenger comfort. The domain of internal-combustion engines also includes such exotic devices as supersonic combustion ramjet engines (scramjets), as typified by the space plane, and sophisticated rocket engines and motors, such as those used on U.S. space shuttles and other space vehicles.

readily available, moderately priced fuel. Reliability, compact size, exhaust emissions, and range of operation later became important factors.

There has been an ongoing reassessment of these priorities with new emphasis on the reduction of greenhouse gases or pollution-producing characteristics of automotive power systems. This has created new interest in alternate power sources and internal-combustion engine refinements that previously were not close to being economically feasible. Several battery-powered electric vehicles are today being marketed. In the past, they have not proved to be competitive, because of costs and operating characteristics. The gasoline engine, with new emission-control devices to improve emission performance, has been challenged in recent years by hybrid power systems that combine gasoline or diesel engines with battery systems and electric motors. Such designs are, however, more complex and therefore more costly.

The evolution of higher-performance engines in the United States led the industry away from long, straight engine cylinder layouts to compact six- and eight-cylinder V-type layouts for larger cars (with horsepower ratings up to about 350). Smaller cars depend on smaller four-cylinder engines. European automobile engines were of a much wider variety, ranging from 1 to 12 cylinders, with corresponding differences in overall size, weight, piston displacement, and cylinder bores. A majority of the models had four cylinders and horsepower ratings up to 120. Most engines had straight or in-line cylinders. There were, however, several V-type models and horizontally opposed two- and four-cylinder makes. Overhead camshafts were frequently employed. The smaller engines were commonly air-cooled and located at the rear of the vehicle; compression ratios were relatively low. Increased

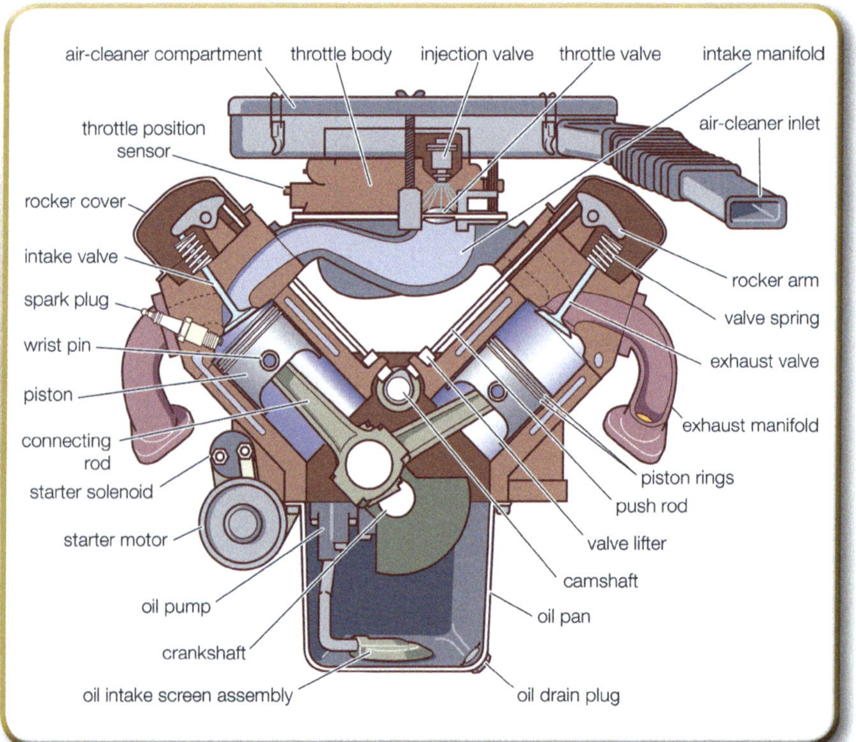

Cross section of a V-type engine. Encyclopædia Britannica, Inc.

interest in improved fuel economy brought a return to smaller V-6 and four-cylinder layouts, with as many as five valves per cylinder to improve efficiency. Variable valve timing to improve performance and lower emissions has been achieved by manufacturers in all parts of the world. Electronic controls automatically select the better of two profiles on the same cam for higher efficiency when engine speeds and loads change.

COOLING SYSTEM

Almost all automobiles employ liquid cooling systems for their engines. A typical automotive cooling system comprises (1) a series of channels cast into the engine block and cylinder head, surrounding the combustion chambers with circulating water or other coolant to carry away excessive heat, (2) a radiator, consisting of many small tubes equipped with a honeycomb of fins to radiate heat rapidly, which receives and cools hot liquid from the engine, (3) a centrifugal-type water pump with which to circulate coolant, (4) a thermostat, which maintains constant temperature by automatically varying the amount of coolant passing into the radiator, and (5) a fan, which draws fresh air through the radiator.

For operation at temperatures below 0 °C (32 °F), it is necessary to prevent the coolant from freezing. This is usually done by adding some compound, such as ethylene glycol, to depress the freezing point of the coolant. By varying the amount of additive, it is possible to protect against freezing of the coolant down to any minimum temperature normally encountered. Coolants contain corrosion inhibitors designed to make it necessary to drain and refill the cooling system only once a year.

Air-cooled cylinders operate at higher, more efficient temperatures, and air cooling offers the important

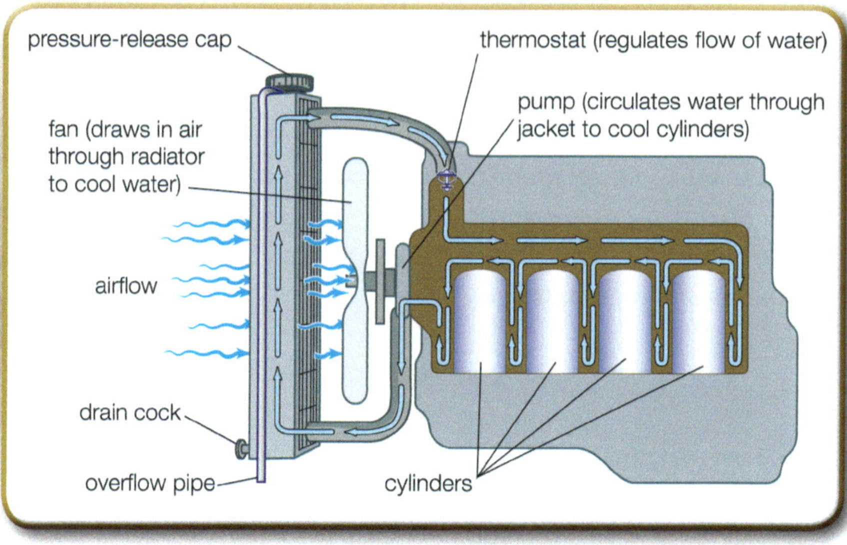

Typical gasoline engine cooling system. Encyclopædia Britannica, Inc.

advantage of eliminating not only freezing and boiling of the coolant at temperature extremes but also corrosion damage to the cooling system. Control of engine temperature is more difficult, however, and high-temperature-resistant ceramic parts are required when design operating temperatures are significantly increased.

Pressurized cooling systems have been used to increase effective operating temperatures. Partially sealed systems using coolant reservoirs for coolant expansion if the engine overheats were introduced in the early 1970s. Specially formulated coolants that do not deteriorate over time eliminate the need for annual replacement.

ELECTRICAL SYSTEM

The electrical system comprises a storage battery, generator, starting (cranking) motor, lighting system, ignition system, and various accessories and controls. Originally, the electrical system of the automobile was limited to the ignition equipment. With the advent of the electric starter on a 1912 Cadillac model, electric lights and horns began to replace the kerosene and acetylene lights and the bulb horns. Electrification was rapid and complete, and, by 1930, 6-volt systems were standard everywhere.

Increased engine speeds and higher cylinder pressures made it increasingly difficult to meet high ignition voltage requirements. The larger engines required higher cranking torque. Additional electrically operated features—such as radios, window regulators, and multispeed windshield wipers—also added to system requirements. To meet these needs, 12-volt systems replaced the 6-volt systems in the late 1950s around the world.

The ignition system provides the spark to ignite the air-fuel mixture in the cylinders of the engine. The system consists of the spark plugs, coil, distributor, and battery. In order to jump the gap between the electrodes of the spark plugs, the 12-volt potential of the electrical system must be stepped up to about 20,000 volts. This is done by a circuit that starts with the battery, one side of which is grounded on the chassis and leads through the ignition switch to the primary winding of the ignition coil and back to the ground through an interrupter switch. Interrupting the primary circuit induces a high voltage across the secondary terminal of the coil. The high-voltage secondary terminal of the coil leads to a distributor that acts as a rotary switch, alternately connecting the coil to each of the wires leading to the spark plugs.

Solid-state or transistorized ignition systems were introduced in the 1970s. These distributor systems provided increased durability by eliminating the frictional contacts between breaker points and distributor cams. The breaker point was replaced by a revolving magnetic-pulse generator in which alternating-current pulses trigger

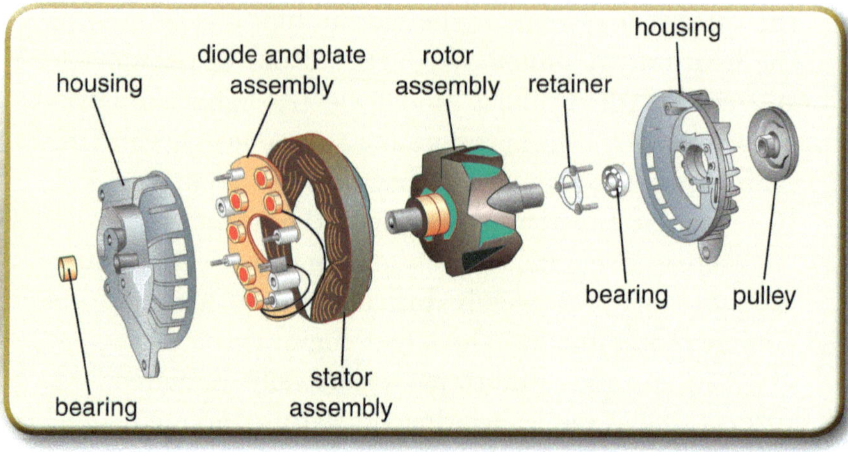

Exploded view of an automotive alternator. © Merriam-Webster Inc.

the high voltage needed for ignition by means of an amplifier electronic circuit. Changes in engine ignition timing are made by vacuum or electronic control unit (microprocessor) connections to the distributor.

The source of energy for the various electrical devices of the automobile is a generator, or alternator, that is belt-driven from the engine crankshaft. The engine's turning crankshaft, connected to the alternator's pulley by a belt, turns the magnetic rotor inside the stationary stator assembly, generating an alternating current. The diode assembly rectifies the alternating current, producing direct current, which is used to meet the demands of the vehicle's electrical system, including recharging the battery. This sequence of events occurs regardless of engine speed.

A lead-acid battery serves as a reservoir to store excess output of the generator. This provides energy for the starting motor and power for operating other electric devices when the engine is not running or when the generator speed is not sufficiently high for the load.

The starting motor drives a small spur gear so arranged that it automatically moves into mesh with gear teeth on the rim of the flywheel as the starting-motor armature begins to turn. When the engine starts, the gear is disengaged, thus preventing damage to the starting motor from overspeeding. The starting motor is designed for high current consumption and delivers considerable power for its size for a limited time.

Headlights must satisfactorily illuminate the highway ahead of the automobile for driving at night or in inclement weather without temporarily blinding approaching drivers. This was achieved in modern cars with double-filament bulbs with a high and a low beam, called sealed-beam units. Introduced in 1940, these bulbs found widespread use following World War II. Such units could have only one filament at the focal point of the reflector. Because of the greater illumination required for high-speed driving with the high beam, the lower beam filament was placed off centre, with a resulting decrease in lighting effectiveness. Separate lamps for these functions can also be used to improve illumination effectiveness.

Dimming is automatically achieved on some cars by means of a photocell-controlled switch in the lamp circuit that is triggered by the lights of an oncoming car. Larger double-filament lamps and halogen-filled lamp bulbs with improved photometrics have permitted a return to two-headlight systems on some cars. Lamp clusters behind aerodynamic plastic covers permitted significant front-end drag reduction and improved fuel economy. In this arrangement, steerable headlights became possible with an electric motor to swivel the lamp assembly in response to steering wheel position. The regulations of various governments dictate brightness and field of view requirements for vehicle lights.

Signal lamps and other special-purpose lights have increased in usage since the 1960s. Amber-coloured front and red rear signal lights are flashed as a turn indication;

all these lights are flashed simultaneously in the "flasher" (hazard) system for use when a car is parked along a roadway or is traveling at a low speed on a high-speed highway. Marker lights that are visible from the front, side, and rear also are widely required by law. Red-coloured rear signals are used to denote braking, and cornering lamps, in connection with turning, provide extra illumination in the direction of an intended turn. Backup lights provide illumination to the rear and warn anyone behind the vehicle when the driver is backing up. High-voltage light-emitting diodes (LEDs) are under development for various signal and lighting applications.

TRANSMISSION

The gasoline engine must be disconnected from the driving wheels when it is started and when idling. This characteristic necessitates some type of unloading and engaging device to permit gradual application of load to the engine after it has been started. The torque, or turning effort, that the engine is capable of producing is low at low crankshaft speeds, increasing to a maximum at some fairly high speed representing the maximum, or rated, horsepower.

The efficiency of an automobile engine is highest when the load on the engine is high and the throttle is nearly wide open. At moderate speeds on level pavement, the power required to propel an automobile is only a fraction of this. Under normal driving conditions at constant moderate speed, the engine may operate at an uneconomically light load unless some means is provided to change its speed and power output.

The transmission is such a speed-changing device. Installed in the power train between the engine and the driving wheels, it permits the engine to operate at a higher

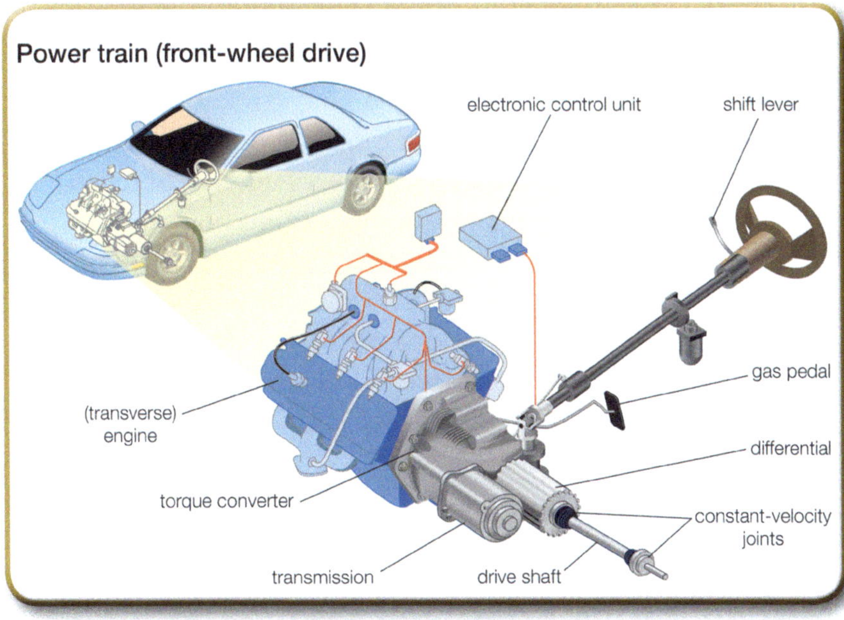

The main elements of the power train of a front-wheel-drive automobile are the transversely mounted engine and the transmission, which transfers the torque, or turning energy, of the engine to the drive wheels through a short drive shaft. Encyclopædia Britannica, Inc.

speed when its full power is needed and to slow down to a more economical speed when less power is needed. Under some conditions, as in starting a stationary vehicle or in ascending steep grades, the torque of the engine is insufficient, and amplification is needed. Most devices employed to change the ratio of the speed of the engine to the speed of the driving wheels multiply the engine torque by the same factor by which the engine speed is increased.

The simplest automobile transmission is the sliding-spur gear type with three or more forward speeds and reverse. The desired gear ratio is selected by manipulating a shift lever that slides a spur gear into the proper position to engage the various gears. A clutch is required to engage and disengage gears during the selection process.

The necessity of learning to operate a clutch is eliminated by an automatic transmission. Most automatic transmissions employ a hydraulic torque converter, a device for transmitting and amplifying the torque produced by the engine. Each type provides for manual selection of reverse and low ranges that either prevent automatic upshifts or employ lower gear ratios than are used in normal driving. Grade-retard provisions are also sometimes included to supply dynamic engine braking on hills. Automatic transmissions not only require little skill to operate but also make possible better performance than is obtainable with designs that require clutch actuation.

In hydraulic transmissions, shifting is done by a speed-sensitive governing device that changes the position of valves that control the flow of hydraulic fluid. The vehicle speeds at which shifts occur depend on the position of the accelerator pedal, and the driver can delay upshifts until higher speed is attained by depressing the accelerator pedal further. Control is by hydraulically engaged bands and multiple-disk clutches running in oil, either by the driver's operation of the selector lever or by speed- and load-sensitive electronic control in the most recent designs. Compound planetary gear trains with multiple sun gears and planet pinions have been designed to provide a low forward speed, intermediate speeds, a reverse, and a means of locking into direct drive. This unit is used with various modifications in almost all hydraulic torque-converter transmissions. All transmission control units are interconnected with vehicle emission control systems that adjust engine timing and air-to-fuel ratios to reduce exhaust emissions.

Oil in the housing is accelerated outward by rotating vanes in the pump impeller and, reacting against vanes in the turbine impeller, forces them to rotate. The oil then passes into the stator vanes, which redirect it to the pump.

The stator serves as a reaction member providing more torque to turn the turbine than was originally applied to the pump impeller by the engine. Thus, it acts to multiply engine torque by a factor of up to 2 ½ to 1.

Blades in all three elements are specially contoured for their specific function and to achieve particular multiplication characteristics. Through a clutch linkage, the stator is allowed gradually to accelerate until it reaches the speed of the pump impeller. During this period torque multiplication gradually drops to approach 1 to 1.

The hydraulic elements are combined with two or more planetary gear sets, which provide further torque multiplication between the turbine and the output shaft.

Continuously (or infinitely) variable transmissions provide a very efficient means of transferring engine power and, at the same time, automatically changing the effective input-to-output ratio to optimize economy by keeping the engine running within its best power range. Most designs employ two variable-diameter pulleys connected by either a steel or high-strength rubber V-belt. The pulleys are split so that effective diameters may be changed by an electro-hydraulic actuator to change the transmission ratio. This permits the electronic control unit to select the optimum ratio possible for maximum fuel economy and minimum emissions at all engine speeds and loads. Originally these units were limited to small cars, but belt improvements have made them suitable for larger cars.

AXLES

Power is conveyed from the transmission to the rear axle of rear-wheel-drive vehicles by a drive shaft and universal joints. As body lines were progressively lowered, the floor level came closer to the drive shaft, necessitating floor humps or tunnels to provide clearance. The adoption of hypoid or offset spiral bevel gears in the rear axle provided an increase in this clearance by lowering the drive pinion below the centre of the axle shafts.

The ring gear of the rear axle surrounds the housing of a differential gear train that serves as an equalizer in dividing the torque between the two driving wheels while permitting one to turn faster than the other when rounding corners. The axle shafts terminate in bevel gears that are connected by several smaller bevel gears mounted on radial axles attached to the differential housing and carried around with it by the ring gear. In its simplest form this differential has the defect that one driving wheel may spin when it loses traction, and the torque applied to the wheel, being equal to that of the slipping wheel, will not be sufficient to drive the car. Several differentials have been developed to overcome this difficulty.

Articulated rear axles offer individual wheel suspension at the rear as well as the front. Individual rear suspension not only eliminates the heavy rear axle housing but also permits lowered bodies with no floor humps, because the transmission and differential gears can be combined in a housing mounted on a rear cross member moving with the body under suspension-spring action. In some instances, articulated or swing axles that have tubular housings surrounding the axle shafts terminate in spherical head segments that fit into matching sockets formed in the sides of the central gear housing. Universal joints within the spherical elements permit the axle shafts to move with the actions of the suspension springs. The gear housing is supported by a rear cross member of the chassis and moves with the sprung portion of the vehicle, as does the drive shaft. Other types eliminate the axle shaft housings and drive the wheels through two open shafts fitted with universal joints. The wheels are then individually supported by radius rods or other suitable linkage. Individually suspended wheels are simplified for rear-engine, rear-wheel-drive cars and front-engine, front-wheel-drive mechanisms. A combined transmission and differential assembly can form a unit with the engine. Two short transverse drive shafts, each having universal joints at both ends, transmit power to the wheels.

BRAKES

Originally, most systems for stopping vehicles were mechanically actuated drum brakes with internally expanding shoes; i.e., foot pressure exerted on the brake pedal was carried directly to semicircular brake shoes by a system of flexible cables. Mechanical brakes, however, were difficult to keep adjusted so that equal braking force was applied at each wheel; and, as vehicle weights and speeds increased, more and more effort on the brake pedal was demanded of the driver.

Mechanical brakes were replaced by hydraulic systems, in which the brake pedal is connected to pistons in master cylinders and thence by steel tubing with flexible sections to individual cylinders at the wheels. Front and rear hydraulic circuits are separated. The wheel cylinders are located between the movable ends of the brake shoes, and each is fitted with two pistons that are forced outward toward the ends of the cylinder by the pressure of the fluid between them. As these pistons move outward, they push the brake shoes against the inner surface of the brake drum attached to the wheel. The larger diameter of the piston in the master cylinder provides a hydraulic force multiplication at the wheel cylinder that reduces the effort required of the driver.

Further increases in vehicle weights and speeds made even hydraulic brakes difficult for drivers to operate effectively, and automobiles consequently were equipped with power brake systems. These are virtually the same as the hydraulic system except that the piston of the master cylinder is multiplied by power assists of several types instead of by foot pressure on the pedal.

Overheating of the brake drums and shoes causes the brakes to fade and lose their effectiveness when held in engagement for a considerable length of time. This problem has been attacked by the use of aluminum cooling fins

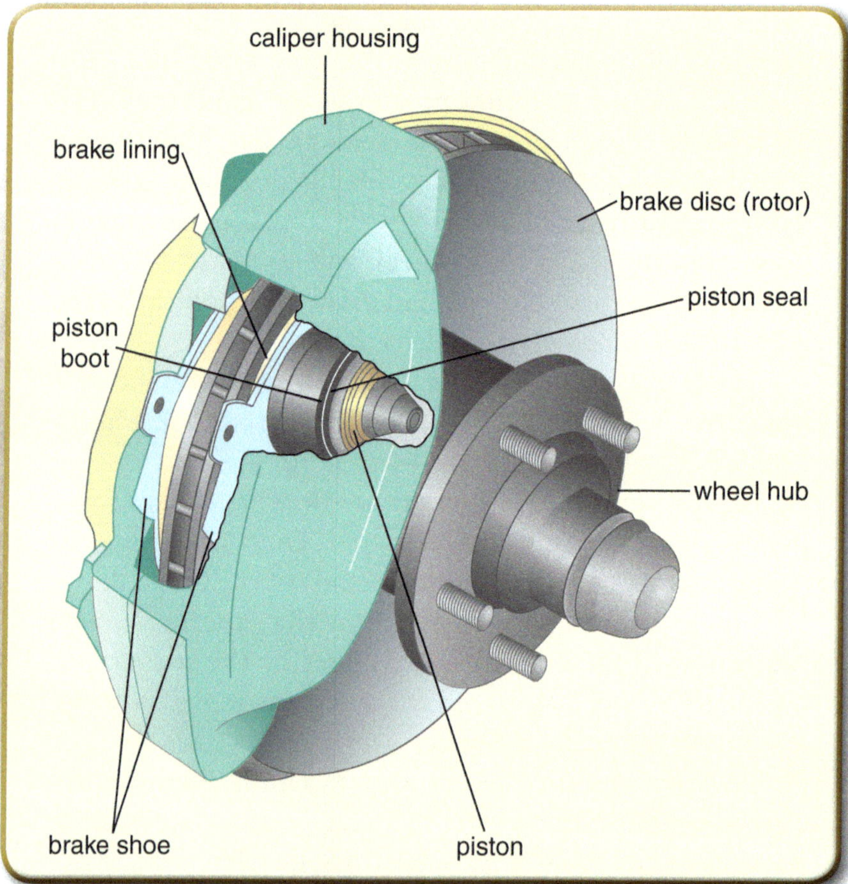

A disc brake assembly. Wheel rotation is slowed by friction when the hydraulic pistons squeeze the caliper, pressing the brake pads (shoe and lining assemblies) against the spinning disc (rotor), which is bolted to the wheel hub. © Merriam-Webster Inc.

bonded to the outside of the brake drums to increase the rate of heat transfer to the air. Vents in the wheels are provided to increase the air circulation for cooling.

Disc brakes, originally developed for aircraft, are ubiquitous, in spite of their higher cost, because of their fade resistance. Although there are some four-wheel systems, usually discs are mounted on the front wheels, and conventional drum units are retained at the rear. They have been standard on most European automobiles since the 1950s and most American models since the mid-1970s. Each wheel has a hub-mounted disc and a brake unit or caliper rigidly attached to the suspension. The caliper employs two friction-pad assemblies, one on each side of the disc. When the brake is applied, hydraulic pressure forces the friction pads against the disc. This arrangement is self-adjusting, and the ability of the discs to dissipate heat rapidly in the open airstream makes them practically immune to fading.

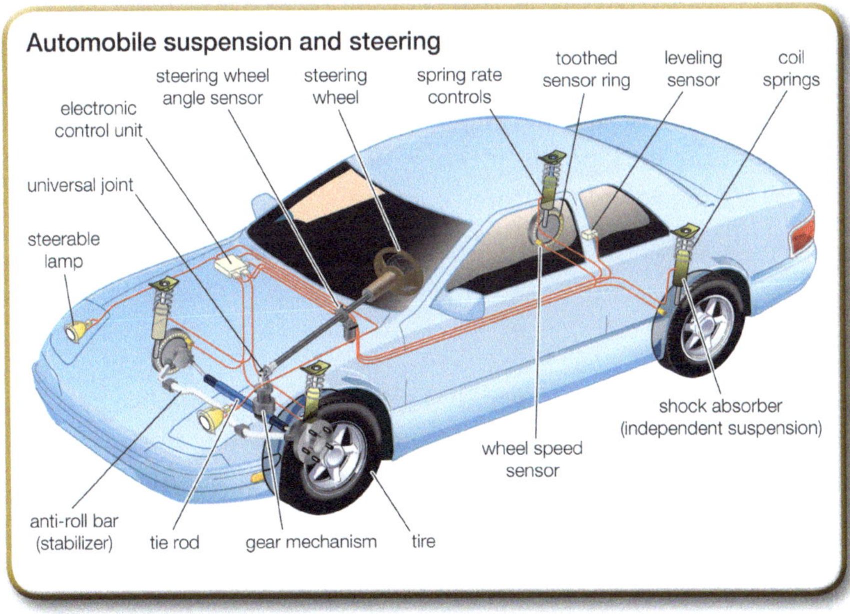

Antilock braking system. Encyclopædia Britannica, Inc.

Antilock braking systems (ABS) became available in the late 1980s and since then have become standard on a growing number of passenger cars. ABS installations consist of wheel-mounted sensors that input wheel rotation speed into a microprocessor. When wheel rotation increases because of tire slippage or loss of traction, the control unit signals a hydraulic or electric modulator to regulate brake line pressure to forestall impending wheel lockup. The brake continues to function as the system cyclically releases and applies pressure, similar to but much faster than a driver rapidly pumping the brake pedal on a non-ABS-equipped automobile. The wheels continue to roll, retaining the driver's ability to steer the vehicle and stop in a shorter distance.

Parking brakes usually are of the mechanical type, applying force only to the rear brake shoes by means of a flexible cable connected to a hand lever or pedal. On cars with automatic transmissions, an additional lock is usually provided in the form of a pawl that can be engaged, by placing the shift lever in the "park" position, to prevent the drive shaft and rear wheels from turning. The service brake pedal must be applied to permit shifting the transmission out of the park position. This eliminates the possibility of undesired vehicle motion that could be caused by accidental movement of the transmission control.

STEERING

Automobiles are steered by a system of gears and linkages that transmit the motion of the steering wheel to the pivoted front wheel hubs. The gear mechanism, located at the lower end of the shaft carrying the steering wheel, is usually a worm-and-nut or cam-and-lever combination that rotates a shaft with an attached crank arm through a small angle as the steering wheel is turned. Tie rods attached to the arm convey its motion to the wheels. In cornering, the inner wheel must turn through a slightly greater angle than the outer wheel because the inner wheel negotiates a sharper turn. The geometry of the linkage is designed to provide for this.

When the front wheels are independently suspended, the steering must be designed so that the wheels are not turned as the tie rods lengthen and shorten as a result of spring action. The point of linkage attachment to the steering gear must be placed so that it can move vertically with respect to the wheel mountings without turning the wheels.

As the engine and passenger compartment in automobiles beginning in the 1930s in Europe and the United States were moved forward to improve riding comfort and road-handling characteristics, the distribution of weight between the front and rear wheels was shifted toward the front. The weight carried on the front wheels increased to more than half of the total vehicle weight, and consequently the effort necessary to turn the wheels in steering increased. Larger, heavier cars with wider tires and lower tire pressure also contributed to drag between tires and road that had to be overcome in steering, particularly in parking. Considerable reduction in the work of steering resulted from increasing the efficiency of the steering gears and introducing better bearings in the front wheel linkage. Additional ease of turning the steering wheel was accomplished by increasing the overall steering gear ratio (the number of degrees of steering-wheel turn required to turn the front wheels one degree). However, large steering gear ratios made high-speed maneuverability more difficult because the steering wheel had to be turned through greater angles. Moreover, steering mechanisms of higher efficiency were also more reversible; that is, road shocks were transmitted more completely from the wheels and had to be overcome to a greater extent by the driver. This caused a dangerous situation on rough roads or when a front tire blew out because the wheel might be jerked from the driver's hands.

Power steering gear was developed to solve the steadily increasing steering problems. Power steering was first applied to heavy trucks and military vehicles early in the 1930s, and hundreds of patents were granted for devices to help the driver turn the steering wheel. Most of the proposed devices were hydraulic; some were electrical and some mechanical. In hydraulic systems, a pump driven by the engine maintains the fluid under pressure. A valve with a sensing device allows the fluid to enter and leave the power cylinder as necessary. Speed-sensitive systems are available to provide larger ratios for reduced effort at low speeds and lower ratios for steering at high speeds. Four-wheel steering systems in which the rear wheels turn in the opposite direction of the front wheels have had limited commercial use.

SUSPENSION

The riding comfort and handling qualities of an automobile are greatly affected by the suspension system, in which the suspended portion of the vehicle is attached to the wheels by elastic members in order to cushion the impact of road irregularities. The specific nature of attaching linkages and spring elements varies widely among automobile models. The best rides are made possible by independent suspension systems, which permit the wheels to move independently of each other. In these systems the unsprung weight of the vehicle is decreased, softer springs are permissible, and front-wheel vibration problems are minimized. Spring elements used for automobile suspension members, in increasing order of their ability to store elastic energy per unit of weight, are leaf springs, coil springs, torsion bars, rubber-in-shear devices, and air springs.

The leaf spring, although comparatively inelastic, has the important advantage of accurately positioning the wheel with respect to the other chassis components, both laterally and fore and aft, without the aid of auxiliary linkages.

An important factor in spring selection is the relationship between load and deflection known as the spring rate, defined as the load in pounds divided by the deflection of the spring in inches. A soft spring has a low rate and deflects a greater distance under a given load. A coil or a leaf spring retains a substantially constant rate within its operating range of load and will deflect 10 times as much if a force 10 times as great is applied to it. The torsion bar, a long spring-steel element with one end held rigidly to the frame and the other twisted by a crank connected to the axle, can be designed to provide an increasing spring rate.

A soft-spring suspension provides a comfortable ride on a relatively smooth road, but the occupants move up and down excessively on a rough road. The springs must be stiff enough to prevent a large deflection at any time because of the difficulty in providing enough clearance between the sprung portion of the vehicle and the unsprung portion below the springs. Lower roof heights make it increasingly difficult to provide the clearance needed for soft springs. Road-handling characteristics also suffer because of what is known as sway, or roll, the sidewise tilting of the car body that results from centrifugal force acting outward on turns. The softer the suspension, the more the outer springs are compressed and the inner springs expanded. In addition, the front end dives more noticeably when braking with soft front springs.

Air springs offer several advantages over metal springs, one of the most important being the possibility of controlling the spring rate. Inherently, the force required to deflect the air unit increases with greater deflection, because the air is compressed into a smaller space and greater pressure is built up, thus progressively resisting further deflection.

A combination hydraulic-fluid-and-air suspension system has been developed in which the elastic medium is a sealed-in, fixed mass of air, and no air compressor is required. The hydraulic portion of each spring is a cylinder mounted on the body sill and fitted with a plunger that is pivotally attached to the wheel linkage to form a hydraulic strut. Each spring cylinder has a spherical air chamber attached to its outer end. The sphere is divided into two chambers by a flexible diaphragm, the upper occupied by air and the lower by hydraulic fluid that is in communication with the hydraulic cylinder through a two-way restrictor valve. This valve limits the rate of movement of the plunger in the cylinder, since fluid must be pushed into the sphere when the body descends and returned when it rises. This damping action thus controls the motion of the wheel with respect to the sprung portion of the vehicle supported by the spring.

So-called active suspensions incorporate a microprocessor to vary the orifice size of the restrictor valve in a hydraulic suspension or shock absorber (a mechanical device that dampens the rate of energy stored and released by the springs). This changes the effective spring rate. Control inputs may be vehicle speed, load, acceleration, lateral force, or a driver preference.

FUEL AND LUBRICATION

Specially formulated gasoline is essentially the only fuel used for automobile operation, although diesel fuels are used for many trucks and buses and a few automobiles, and compressed liquefied hydrogen is being used experimentally. The most important requirements of a fuel for automobile use are proper volatility, sufficient antiknock quality, and freedom from polluting by-products of combustion. The volatility is reformulated seasonally by refiners so that sufficient gasoline vaporizes, even in extremely cold weather, to permit easy engine starting. Antiknock quality is rated by the octane number of the gasoline. The octane number requirement of an automobile engine depends primarily on the compression ratio of the engine but is also affected by combustion-chamber design, the maintenance condition of engine systems, and chamber-wall deposits. In the 21st century regular gasoline carried an octane rating of 87 and high-test in the neighbourhood of 93.

Automobile manufacturers have lobbied for regulations that require the refinement of cleaner-burning gasolines, which permit emission-control devices to work at higher efficiencies. Such gasoline was first available at some service stations in California, and since 2005 the primary importers and refiners of gasoline throughout the United States were required to remove sulfur particles from fuel to an average level of 30 parts per million (ppm).

Vehicle fleets fueled by natural gas have been in operation for years. Carbon monoxide and particulate emissions are reduced by 65 to 90 percent. Natural-gas fuel tanks must be four times larger than gasoline tanks for equivalent vehicles to have the same driving range. This compromises cargo capacity.

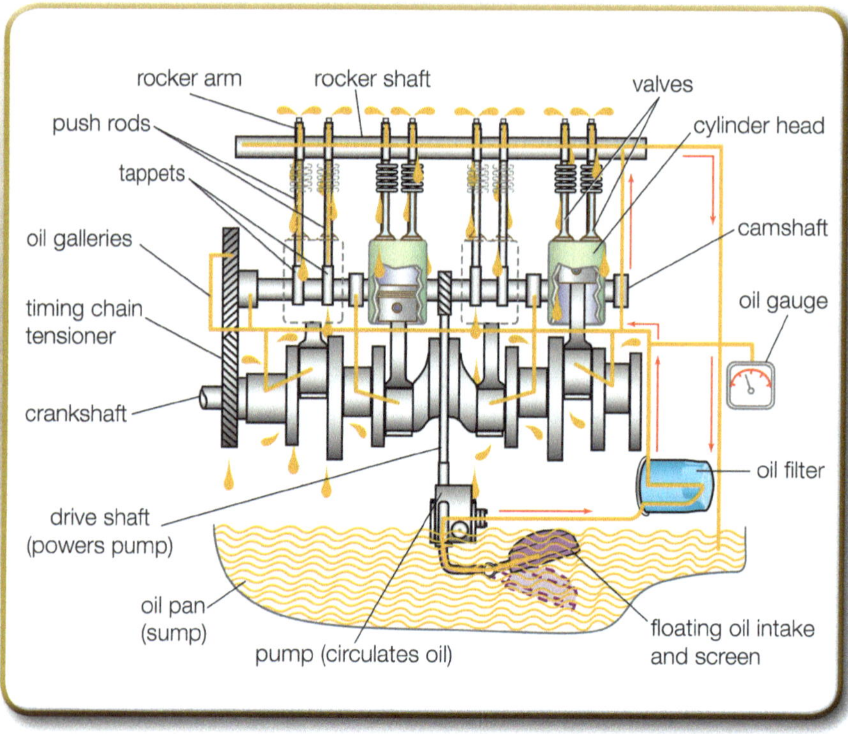

Typical gasoline engine lubrication system. Encyclopædia Britannica, Inc.

Ethanol (ethyl alcohol) is often blended with gasoline (15 parts to 85 parts) to raise its octane rating, which results in a smoother-running engine. Ethanol, however, has a lower energy density than gasoline, which results in decreased range per tankful.

All moving parts of an automobile require lubrication. Without it, friction would increase power consumption and damage the parts. The lubricant also serves as a coolant, a noise-reducing cushion, and a sealant between engine piston rings and cylinder walls. The engine lubrication system incorporates a gear-type pump that delivers filtered oil under pressure to a system of drilled passages leading to various bearings. Oil spray also lubricates the cams and valve lifters.

Wheel bearings and universal joints require a fairly stiff grease; other chassis joints require a soft grease that can be injected by pressure guns. Hydraulic transmissions require a special grade of light hydraulic fluid, and manually shifted transmissions use a heavier gear oil similar to that for rear axles to resist heavy loads on the gear teeth. Gears and bearings in lightly loaded components, such as generators and window regulators, are fabricated from self-lubricating plastic materials. Hydraulic fluid is also used in other vehicle systems in conjunction with small electric pumps and motors.

TIRES

The pneumatic rubber tire is the point of contact between the automobile and the road surface. It functions to provide traction for acceleration and braking and limits the transmission of road vibrations to the automobile body. Inner tubes within tires were standard until the 1950s, when seals between the tire and the wheel were developed, leading to tubeless tires, now used almost universally.

Tire tread designs are tailored for the characteristics of the surface on which the vehicle is intended to operate. Deep designs provide gripping action in loose soil and snow, while smooth surfaces provide maximum contact area for applications such as racing. Current passenger car treads are a compromise between these extremes.

A typical tire casing is fabricated from layers, or plies, of varying proportions of rubber compounds reinforced with synthetic and carbon fibres or steel wire. The composition of the reinforcement and the angle of its application to the axis of the tread affect the ability of the tire to respond to sidewise forces created during cornering. They also affect harshness or vibration-transmission characteristics.

By 1990, longitudinal-, bias-, and radial-ply constructions were in use, with layers of two, four, or more plies, depending on the load capacity of the design. An additional factor relating to the load capacity of a particular construction is the pressure to which the tire is inflated. New designs also have lower height-to-width ratios to increase the road-contact area while maintaining a low standing height for the tire and consequently the car.

SECURITY SYSTEMS

Motor vehicle theft has been a problem since the start of the automobile age. The 1900 Leach automobile featured a removable steering wheel that the driver could carry away to prevent unauthorized vehicle use. More recently, sophisticated electronic alarms, some of which incorporate radio beacons, and more tamper-resistant wiring and electronic locks have been produced. Through the use of wireless technology, vehicles equipped with Global Positioning System (GPS) satellite navigation systems may be tracked and recovered when stolen.

SAFETY SYSTEMS

From its beginnings the automobile posed serious hazards to public safety. Vehicle speed and weight provided an impact capacity for occupants and pedestrians that produced great numbers of fatalities (13,000 in 1920 in the United States alone and many more in Europe, as well as many serious injuries). During the 20th century the rates of death and injury declined significantly in terms of vehicle miles. Because of the increased number of vehicles on the road, total fatalities declined only slightly. However, since 2005, fatalities have declined by 25 percent for reasons that are not understood. Most fatal accidents occur on either city streets or secondary roads. New divided roadway designs are relatively safer. Driver training, vehicle maintenance, highway improvement, and law enforcement have been identified as key areas responsible for improving safety, but the basic design of the vehicle itself and the addition of special safety features were significant factors in worldwide reduction of fatal accidents. Rates vary from country to country. Safety features of automobiles come under two distinct headings: accident avoidance and occupant protection.

Accident-avoidance systems are designed to help the driver maintain better control of the car. The dual-master-cylinder brake system is a good example. This protects the driver against sudden loss of brake line pressure. Front and rear brake lines are separated so that if one fails, the other will continue to function.

Systems for protecting occupants in the event of an accident fall into four major classes: maintenance of passenger-compartment integrity, occupant restraints, interior-impact energy-absorber systems, and exterior-impact energy absorbers. Statistics indicate a far higher chance for survival among accident victims remaining inside the passenger compartment. Passenger-compartment integrity depends significantly on the proper action of the doors, which must remain closed in the event of an accident and must be sufficiently secure to prevent intrusion. Door-latch mechanisms have been designed to resist forward, rearward, and sideward forces and incorporate two-stage catches, so that the latch may hold if the primary stage fails. Reinforcement beams in doors are designed to deflect impact forces downward to the more rigid frame structure below the door. Forces are directed through reinforced door pillars and hinges.

Occupant restraints are used to help couple the passenger to the car. They permit decelerating with the car rather than free flight into the car structure or into the air. A combination of lap and shoulder belts is the most common restraint system. The belts consist of web fabrics that are required by regulations in various countries to withstand 2,700-kg (6,000-pound) test loading and are bolted to the car underbody and roof rail. Button-type latch release mechanisms are provided for buckles.

Another line of engineering development has centred on passive restraints that do not require any action by the occupant. In particular, commercial air bags were introduced in the 1980s, and all new automobiles sold in the United States since 1998 (1999 for light trucks) have required both driver and front passenger air bags. When a vehicle equipped with an air bag undergoes a "hard" impact, roughly in excess of 16 km (10 miles) per hour, a crash sensor sends an electrical signal that triggers an explosion that generates nitrogen gas to inflate air bags located in the steering column, front dashboard, and possibly other locations. Air bags burst from their locations and inflate to a position between occupants and the car structure in less than one-tenth of a second. The inflated air bags absorb impact energy from occupants by forcing gas out through a series of ports or orifices in the air bag fabric. Air bags collapse in about one second, thereby allowing occupants to exit the vehicle.

It has been estimated that 46 percent of front-seat fatalities could be eliminated by air bags when they are used in conjunction with lap or lap-and-shoulder belts. This is a 10 percent improvement over the use of lap and shoulder belt systems alone. The front-mounted air bag does not provide protection in side or rear crashes or in prolonged impacts from rollovers. Additional side-mounted air bags, however, provide a measure of protection in side impacts and are available in some vehicle models.

Interior-impact energy-absorbing devices augment restraint systems by absorbing energy from the occupant while minimizing injuries. The energy-absorbing steering column, introduced in 1967, is a good example of such a device. Instrument panels, windshield glass, and other surfaces that may be struck by an unrestrained occupant may be designed to absorb energy in a controlled manner.

Exterior-impact energy-absorbing devices include the structural elements of the chassis and body, which may be tailored to deform in a controlled manner to decelerate the automobile more gradually and, as a result, leave less force to be experienced by the occupants. Stress risers in the form of section irregularities have been built into front frame members of some cars. These are designed to buckle under severe loads and absorb energy in the process.

EMISSION CONTROLS

By-products of the operation of the gasoline engine include carbon monoxide, oxides of nitrogen, and hydrocarbons (unburned fuel compounds), each of which is a pollutant. To control the air pollution resulting from these emissions, governments establish quality standards and perform inspections to ensure that standards are met. Standards have become progressively more stringent, and the equipment necessary to meet them has become more complex.

Various engine modifications that alter emission characteristics have been successfully introduced. These include adjusted air-fuel ratios, lowered compression ratios, retarded spark timing, reduced combustion chamber surface-to-volume ratios, and closer production tolerances. To improve drivability ("responsiveness") of some arrangements, preheated air from a heat exchanger on the exhaust manifold is ducted to the air cleaner.

The undesired evaporation of gasoline hydrocarbons into the air has been controlled by sealing the fuel tank and venting the tank through a liquid-vapour separator into a canister containing activated charcoal. During engine operation these vapours are desorbed and burned in the engine.

Among emission-control devices developed in the 1970s were catalytic converters (devices to promote combustion of hydrocarbons in the exhaust), exhaust-gas-recirculation systems, manifold reactors, fuel injection, and unitized ignition elements.

A catalytic converter consists of an insulated chamber containing a porous bed, or substrate, coated with catalytic material through which hot exhaust gas must pass before being discharged into the air. The catalyst is one of a variety of metal oxides, usually platinum or palladium, which are heated by exhaust gas to about 500 °C (900 °F). At this temperature unburned hydrocarbons and carbon monoxide are further oxidized, while oxides of nitrogen are chemically reduced in a second chamber with a different catalyst. Problems with catalysts involve their intolerance for leaded fuels and the need to prevent overheating.

Exhaust-gas recirculation is a technique to control oxides of nitrogen, which are formed by the chemical reaction of nitrogen and oxygen at high temperatures during combustion. Either reducing the concentrations of these elements or lowering peak cycle temperatures will reduce the amount of nitrogen oxides produced. To achieve this, exhaust gas is piped from the exhaust manifold to the intake manifold. This dilutes the incoming fuel-air mixture and effectively lowers combustion temperature. The amount of recirculation is a function of throttle position but averages about 2 percent.

Manifold reactors are enlarged and insulated exhaust manifolds into which air is injected and in which exhaust gas continues to burn. The effectiveness of such units depends on the amount of heat generated and the length of time the gas is within the manifold. Stainless steel and ceramic materials are used to provide durability at high operating temperatures (approaching 1,300 °C [about 2,300 °F]).

Fuel injection, as a replacement for carburetion, is almost universally employed to reduce exhaust emissions. The precise metering of fuel for each cylinder provides a means of ensuring that the chemically correct air-to-fuel ratio is being burned in the engine. This eliminates cylinder-to-cylinder variations and the tendency of cylinders that are most remote from the carburetor to receive less fuel than is desired. A variety of metering and control systems are commercially available. Timed injection, in which a small quantity of gasoline is squirted into each cylinder or intake-valve port during the intake stroke of the piston, is employed on a number of cars.

In several timed-injection systems, individual pumps at each intake valve are regulated (timed) by a microprocessor that monitors intake vacuum, engine temperature, ambient-air temperature, and throttle position and adjusts the time and duration of injection accordingly.

EXPERIMENTAL SYSTEMS

The U.S. automotive industry spends billions of dollars on research and development of future products in a typical year—the most spent by any industry in the United States. Increasing pressure from various governments is requiring manufacturers to develop very low- and zero-emission vehicles. Authorities in California estimate that motor vehicles produce 40 percent of the greenhouse gases that they consider to be responsible for climate change. To meet this challenge, manufacturers are working on a timetable to produce more efficient vehicle designs.

Expansion of the total potential automotive market in the future and concern for the environment may be expected to change cars of the future. Special-purpose vehicles designed for specific urban or rural functions, with appropriate power systems for each type of use, may be needed. Possibilities include solar, steam, gas turbine, new hybrid combinations, and other power sources.

Steam power plants have been reexamined in the light of modern technology and new materials. The continuous-combustion process used to heat the steam generator offers potentially improved emission characteristics.

Gas turbines have been tested extensively and have good torque characteristics, operate on a wide variety of fuels, have high power-to-weight ratios, meet emission standards, and offer quiet operation. Some studies have shown that the advantages of the system are best realized in heavy-duty vehicles operating on long, nearly constant speed runs. Efficiencies and operating characteristics can be improved by increasing operating temperatures. This may become commercially feasible utilizing ceramic materials that are cost-effective. Successful designs require regenerative systems to recover energy from hot exhaust gas and transfer it to incoming air. This improves fuel economy, reduces exhaust temperatures to safer levels, and eliminates the need for a muffler in some designs.

A number of other designs have been studied involving variations of engine combustion cycles such as turbocharged gasoline and diesel (two- and four-stroke) designs. Rotary engines have been produced in Germany and Japan, but they have been discontinued, except in the Mazda RX-8, because of exhaust emission control complexity. Variable valve timing can optimize performance and economy and provide a more constant engine torque output at different engine speeds. By delaying the opening of the engine exhaust valve, exhaust gas is effectively recirculated to reduce tailpipe emissions. Electro-hydraulic valves that totally replace the complexity of camshaft designs, or idlers that may be moved to change the geometry of the camshaft timing chain and retard valve opening, may be used for this purpose.

Solar-powered electric demonstration vehicles have been built by universities and manufacturers. Solar collector areas have proved to be too large for conventional cars, however. Development continues on solar cell design.

Microprocessors have become increasingly important in improving fuel economy and reducing undesirable exhaust emissions for all vehicle types. Research to develop so-called intelligent vehicles that can assist the driver and even operate without driver intervention, at least on special roads, has made some progress. These developments have been made possible by highly reliable solid-state digital computers and similarly reliable electronic sensors. The automobile industry has worked with governmental bodies to link vehicles to their environments using advanced telecommunication signals, electronic systems, and digital computers, both within the vehicle and aboard satellites and in other remote locations. Applications may be divided into functions for basic vehicle system assistance, safety and security applications, and information and entertainment systems.

The automobile industry is responsible for about two-thirds of the rubber, one-half of the platinum, one-third of the aluminum, one-seventh of the steel, and one-tenth of the copper consumed in the United States each year. About three-quarters of the material in a car is recyclable, and in the United States 19 out of 20 scrapped cars are recycled. Because the automobile is likely to remain an important part of the transportation system, it requires continuing improvement in safety and emission control as well as performance and cost.

CHAPTER 4

Trucks and Buses

The wagons and carriages of the 19th century have their equivalents in the trucks and buses of today. However, their use of the internal-combustion engine allow trucks and buses to carry more goods and more people than their horse-drawn predecessors could.

TRUCKS

The truck was derived from horse-driven wagon technology, and some of the pioneer manufacturers came from the wagon business. In 1896 Gottlieb Daimler of Germany built the first motor truck. It was equipped with a four-horsepower engine and a belt drive with two speeds forward and one in reverse. In 1898 the Winton Company of the United States produced a gasoline-powered delivery wagon with a single-cylinder six-horsepower engine.

In World War I motor trucks were widely used, and in World War II they largely replaced horse-drawn equipment. A notable vehicle was the four-wheel-drive, quarter-ton-capacity, short-wheelbase jeep, capable of performing a variety of military tasks.

Because of well-developed systems of modern roads and highways in North America and Europe, trucks have come to carry most intercity freight, with the exception of bulk materials such as ores, which are typically still carried by ship and rail, and time-critical deliveries, which are usually carried between cities by air. Trucks enjoy an almost total monopoly in intracity freight delivery because of their ability to deliver goods directly to recipients.

In the last quarter of the 20th century, new truck sales grew tremendously in the United States. In large part this happened because of the introduction of utility and sport utility vehicles, which are classified as light trucks but operated as family vehicles. Light trucks accounted for more than 90 percent of all truck sales and roughly half of total vehicle sales in the United States annually by the start of the 21st century. This phenomenon was unique to the American market; worldwide, trucks are purchased mainly for commercial operation.

TYPES OF TRUCKS

Trucks can be classified as either straight or articulated. A straight truck is one in which all axles are attached to a single frame. An articulated vehicle is one that consists of two or more separate frames connected by suitable couplings. A truck tractor is a motor vehicle designed primarily for drawing truck trailers and constructed to carry part of the weight and load of a semitrailer, which is a truck trailer equipped with one or more axles and constructed so that the end and a substantial part of its own weight and that of its load rests upon a truck tractor. In contrast, a full trailer is constructed so that all of its own weight and that of its load rests upon its own wheels.

A device called a fifth wheel is used to connect a truck tractor to a semitrailer and to permit articulation between the units. It generally includes a lower half, consisting of a trunnion (pivot assembly) plate and latching mechanism, mounted on the truck tractor for connection with a kingpin mounted on the semitrailer. A semitrailer may be converted to a full trailer by a trailer-converter dolly, an

A tractor truck fifth wheel, displaying the trunnion plate with a notch for a semitrailer kingpin, or hitch. Shutterstock.com

auxiliary axle assembly equipped with the lower half of a fifth wheel, a drawbar, and other special parts.

Axle assemblies of heavy trucks may be made up of two or more axles, any of which may be powered. Normally, they are spaced so that the distance between axle centres is not more than one and one-half times the overall diameter of the wheel and tire. If the axles are separated by a larger distance, the assembly is called a spread tandem.

Trucks are organized for regulatory purposes in the United States by their fully loaded capacity, or gross vehicle weight (GVW) rating. Light trucks have GVW ratings that do not exceed 10,000 pounds (4.5 metric tons); GVWs of less than 8,500 pounds (3.9 metric tons) are classified as work trucks. These vehicles generally have more in common with passenger cars than with larger trucks. More than half of the world production of trucks consists of light pickup trucks, utility vehicles, and vans. Medium trucks have GVW ratings of 10,000 to 26,000 pounds (4.5 to 11.8 metric tons) and are generally straight designs. They make up about 3 percent of sales. Heavy-duty haulers with GVW ratings of more than 26,000 pounds are cross-country tractor-trailer combinations and off-road construction or mining trucks; these account for the remainder. A small number of off-road vehicles have GVW ratings that exceed 80,000 pounds (36.3 metric tons). About 15 million trucks are added to the world total each year, but since 2004 the ratio of trucks to passenger cars in the world has decreased annually.

Truck operators are taxed and regulated by government agencies. Approximately half of the revenues that are collected from federal and state highway users in the United States come from the trucking industry. Regulations limit the permissible length, height, weight, safety standards, speed, and noise and exhaust emission levels. Standards are generally similar to those for passenger cars.

Between 150,000 and 400,000 recreational vehicles (RVs) are produced each year in the United States, depending on economic conditions. These are primarily vans and panel trucks that are modified by RV manufacturers. Half of the units are trailers that are not self-propelled. The majority of these are attached to cars and trucks by a ball-type hitch. A portion, however, are towed by light trucks with fifth-wheel hitches mounted on the truck bed. This arrangement permits greater loading on the hitch. Motor homes built on truck chassis that have been supplied by major truck manufacturers to the builders account for the balance of recreational vehicle production.

A self-propelled motor home, displaying the truck chassis upon which the remainder of the vehicle was designed and built. Shutterstock.com

Truck aerodynamics is important for efficient high-speed highway transportation. Cab designs include extended surfaces that smooth the flow of air over and around the truck and trailer bodies and baffle air flow under the truck to reduce drag and lower the cost of truck operation. Narrowing the space between the truck cab and the trailer has a similar effect. Total operating cost savings of 22 percent have been projected for improved truck aerodynamics.

TRUCK SYSTEMS

Like automobiles, trucks work through the interaction of many different mechanical systems. However, trucks are not merely large automobiles. They have their own unique requirements.

TRUCK FRAMES

Truck and truck-tractor frames, except for the very small sizes, have remained separate from the cab and body. The frame is generally made of two channel sections of alloy steel with a standardized width of 86 cm (34 inches) overall. Semitrailers and tank trailers in many instances now employ the integral, or unitized, type of construction. An increasing number of trailer frames are designed to permit the mounting of standardized shipping containers in place of trailer bodies. These units are designed for the more efficient intermodal shipping of products by ship, rail, and trucks, without the need for unloading goods at transfer points.

SUSPENSION SYSTEMS

The most common form of front suspension is a drop-forged, one-section front axle attached to the frame through leaf springs and shock absorbers. In 1960 individual front suspension was introduced.

In a truck with a single powered axle, the axle is generally attached to the frame by leaf springs. The axle is always full-floating with the weight carried by the axle housing so that, if a driving axle breaks, the load is still supported by the axle housing. The axle may be a single reduction type, meaning that it has one-gear reduction, or double reduction. A two-speed axle is one in which there is a gear change built into the axle. This makes it possible to have two speeds for each transmission speed. The tandem-drive axle has two powered axles. There may be two drive shafts, one to each axle. There is always a system of levers between the two axles to equalize the load. A powered axle may be either the Hotchkiss type, in which all the driving and braking thrust is taken by the leaf springs, or the torque-arm type, in which the thrusts are taken by the rods. Because the vertical movement of the body is only one-half that of the wheels in a tandem axle, this axle is used successfully with solid rubber springs, reducing maintenance.

STEERING

Steering of trucks, with their relatively heavy loads, was a problem until power steering came into use in the early

NOISE AND EMISSIONS CONTROL

Under the Clean Air Act Amendments of 1990, which was published as a final rule on June 5, 1991, the United States set a schedule for progressive improvements in truck emissions (based on vehicle weight and engine type) between 1994 and 1997. On Dec. 21, 1999, a new schedule was adopted, known as the Tier 2 standards (with the earlier provisions termed Tier 1), which was phased in between 2004 and 2009. California emission standards typically precede the federal levels by two years. The European Union also adopted a series of emission standards, starting with Euro 1 in 1994, with Euro 6 set for enforcement in 2014 or 2015 depending on truck class.

Modern trucks are easily recognized as a source of noise pollution. The major sources of noise, in decreasing significance, are tire-road contact, engine exhaust, and cooling ducts and fans. The decibel level of each may be reduced by changing tire-tread designs and highway surfaces, by improving exhaust muffler efficiency and shielding the engine with more absorbent materials, and by changing fan blade and engine enclosure designs. The U.S. Society of Automotive Engineers (SAE), which sets a wide variety of test procedures for motor vehicles, has developed standard tests for measuring noise levels, and many different federal, state, and local authorities in the United States have enacted 80-decibel noise limits based on SAE tests. Similar regulations exist within the European Union.

1950s. Steering is always by the Ackermann system, which provides a kingpin for each front wheel. Maximum cramp angle of the front wheels is about 35 degrees. The minimum turning radius is dependent on the wheelbase. A few vehicles have been built with two steering axles in the front.

ENGINES

Until the 1930s the gasoline engine was widely used for trucks, especially in the United States, but since World War II the diesel engine has become increasingly favoured for trucks used for long-distance hauls. In 1950 the Boeing Company installed a gas turbine in a truck, but such designs have not been commercially acceptable. In 1952 an engine using liquefied propane gas was introduced. While the diesel engine has the disadvantage of high initial cost, the propane-burning engine has the disadvantage of lower output for a given engine displacement.

TIRES

Although pneumatic tires appeared on automobiles as early as 1904, large trucks were equipped with hard rubber tires until World War I. Cotton was replaced by synthetics in the carcass of truck tires in the 1930s, with steel wire and fibreglass plies appearing later. In the 1990s the use of a single wide tire to carry the same load as a dual wheel became common. Tire chains first became available in 1904 and knobby snow tires by 1936. To reduce costs, many trucking firms use recapped tires, extending the life of the carcass about two and a half times. In 1955 tubeless tires became available in large truck sizes.

TRANSMISSIONS

Automatic transmissions for trucks have been available since the 1950s. For some diesels it is necessary to operate the engine within a relatively narrow speed range. This requires a large number of forward speeds, with some units having as many as 18 speeds.

BRAKES

The first truck brakes were brake shoes operating directly on the wheels. From this simple beginning has evolved one of the most complex braking systems found on any type of vehicle. The first air brakes were introduced in 1918. Seven years later four-wheel brakes were introduced on trucks, and the internally expanding type was introduced by 1930. In the late 1930s the vacuum booster, or hydraulic brake, was introduced. In electric brake systems a floating armature contacts a rotating disk on the wheel when electric current is applied and through a cam arrangement applies the shoes to the drums. Air-over-hydraulic brakes also are used in some vehicles.

Of these methods of application, air is the most widely used. The engine-driven compressor supplies air at a nominal pressure, regulated by an air governor. Air pressure is indicated by a pressure gauge and a low-pressure warning device, either audible or visual. Air is stored in the reservoirs and supplied to the brake valves; a foot valve supplies air to all brake chambers on the vehicle, including those being towed. Another brake valve is hand-controlled and applies the brakes on the towed vehicle only. Both the foot pedal and hand valve supply air to the same service line, which extends back to the towed vehicles. The second, or emergency, line carries full air pressure when the vehicle is in operation. If this line is broken, the emergency brakes are applied on all towed vehicles from air reservoirs located on the towed vehicles. After reaching the brake chamber from the brake valves, the air acts on a diaphragm connected to a push rod, which in turn actuates a cam or wedge that moves the shoes against the brake drum. Other emergency brake application systems utilize the parking brake circuitry and a mechanical spring to keep the brakes engaged in the event of air pressure loss. These are operated by controls in the truck cab.

BUSES

Buses are large, self-propelled, wheeled vehicles that are designed to carry passengers, generally on a fixed route. They were developed at the beginning of the 20th century to compete with streetcars by providing greater route flexibility. The bus was a natural outgrowth of the horse-driven coach. Today buses are defined as vehicles that accommodate more than 10 passengers.

DEVELOPMENT

In 1830 Sir Goldworthy Gurney of Great Britain designed a large stagecoach driven by a steam engine that may have been the first motor-driven bus. In 1895 an eight-passenger omnibus, driven by a four-horsepower single-cylinder engine, was built in Germany. Early buses in the United States were operated by sightseeing companies in New York City. One type of these open vehicles built by Mack Trucks, Inc., in 1904 had a nominal seating capacity of 15 with a four-cylinder gasoline engine developing 36 horsepower at street speeds of up to 32 km (20 miles) per hour.

Until the 1920s the technical history of the bus was that of the motor truck because the early bus consisted of a bus body mounted on a truck chassis. In 1921 the first vehicle with a chassis specifically designed for bus service was made in the United States by Fageol Safety Coach

Company of Oakland, Calif. The widened and lengthened frame was 30 cm (12 inches) lower than a truck frame. In 1926 Fageol developed the first integral-frame bus, with twin engines mounted amidships under the floor. The integral frame utilized the roof, floor, and sides of the bus as structural members.

Other early bus manufacturers were Mack and Yellow Truck & Coach in the United States, both of which built gasoline-electric models. In these buses a gasoline engine drove a direct-current generator, and the output of the generator provided electrical power for the driving motors on the rear wheels. In 1928 transcontinental bus service was initiated in the United States. In 1931 the first rear engine in an integral-frame bus was introduced. Two-stroke-cycle diesel engines were first used in buses in 1938 and are still found in most city and intercity models.

Air suspensions were introduced in 1953 and continue to be employed on integral-frame bus models. They consist of multiple heavy rubber bellows, or air springs, mounted at each axle. The air springs are supplied with air from a reservoir in which the pressure is maintained at about 690 kilopascals (100 pounds per square inch). An advantage gained from this type of suspension is that, as the load increases or decreases, the level and height of the vehicle remain constant. This is accomplished by valves that increase pressure in the air spring. The increased unit pressure multiplied by a nearly constant area gives a greater load capacity.

Unlike the leaf spring but like the coil spring, the air spring is capable of withstanding only vertical forces. Consequently, braking and cornering forces must be absorbed by radius rods. These are sets of links or arms with one end attached to the axle housing and the other end jointed to attach to the body.

Luggage being loaded onto a bus. Transit and intercity buses are designed with high-ride platforms to accommodate luggage compartments below. © Nordic Photos/SuperStock

MODERN BUSES

There are four main types of buses: city or transit, suburban, intercity or tour, and school. The city bus operates within the city limits and is characterized by low maximum speed, low-ride platform, provision for standing and wheelchair passengers, two entrances on the curb side, low-back seats, and no luggage space. The suburban bus is designed for short intercity runs and has high-back seats, luggage compartments and racks, and a single, front entrance. The intercity type has a high-ride platform to provide maximum luggage space under the passengers, high-back seats, overhead luggage racks, television monitors, individual reading light and ventilation controls, and a restroom. A typical intercity coach weighs about 12,000 kg (26,000 pounds), has a capacity of up to 47 passengers,

GREYHOUND LINES, INC.

Greyhound has provided the major intercity bus transportation in the United States and Canada. The company traces to 1925–26, when Eric Wickman and Orville S. Caesar, intercity bus operators, joined forces, acquired financing, and merged several bus companies into the Motor Transit Management. Some of the early backers were the railroads, first the Great Northern Railroad and then the Southern Pacific, Pennsylvania, and New York Central railroads. A network of lines quickly spread across the country, through purchase of existing companies and inauguration of new lines. In 1930 Motor Transit officially became Greyhound Corporation, with the "running dog" as its trademark. By 1933 Greyhound had routes totaling 65,000 km (40,000 miles). In 1961, however, a policy decision was made to diversify; and in the succeeding decades the company became a conglomerate, expanding into several new products and services, such as toiletries and household-products manufacturing, catering, airport-terminal services, and financial services. (From 1970 to 1983 it also owned the meat-packing Armour & Company.) Greyhound's business operations became international.

In the early 1980s deregulation of the bus-transit industry caused Greyhound Corporation to drop many of its local bus routes, isolating many small towns in rural United States. In 1987 the Greyhound Corporation (which was later renamed Greyhound Dial Corporation), based in Phoenix, Ariz., sold its historic bus operations. Greyhound Lines, Inc., based in Dallas, became an independent corporation devoted entirely to intercity bus transportation. In 1999 Greyhound merged with the Canadian bus company Laidlaw, Inc., which was subsequently purchased in 2007 by the British transit operator FirstGroup PLC.

a two-stroke-cycle V-8 diesel engine with up to 450 horsepower, an electronically controlled automatic transmission, and air brakes. School buses generally consist of a 50-passenger bus body, with special signal lamp and safety provisions, mounted on a long-wheelbase truck chassis. As fuel costs increased during the 1990s and 2000s, bus ridership increased in many urban regions around the world.

Articulated buses were first used in Europe in the 1950s. In this arrangement a trailer body is connected to the rear of a conventional front-engine bus by means of a hitch, a flexible diaphragm, and a continuous floor panel with arcuate mating surfaces during turn maneuvers. This arrangement permits up to a 75 percent increase in seating capacity and a 20 percent improvement in fuel efficiency per seat-kilometre. The turning radius is the same as that of a conventional bus. Manufacture of this design was begun in the United States in the 1980s by several European firms. Double decking, increased seating comfort, and larger glass areas have been trends in tour buses, principally in Europe and Asia.

A typical cross-country bus has been estimated to remove 17 cars from the highway and to achieve 69 passenger-km per litre (162 passenger-miles per gallon). Experimental hybrid-electric bus designs are being built, based on automobile practice. Intermodal transit systems with coordinated bus, train, and private car continue to be studied because of their efficiency and pollution reduction potential.

New exhaust emission standards for buses went into effect in the United States in 2006 and 2007, requiring that smog-related emissions be reduced by 95 percent and soot by 90 percent relative to 2000 levels. The reductions required a switch to reformulated diesel fuels with sulfur content capped at 15 parts per million.

CHAPTER 5

Motorcycles and Bicycles

Both motorcycles and bicycles were invented in the 19th century. They have proved to be popular recreational vehicles ever since.

MOTORCYCLES

Any two-wheeled or, less commonly, three-wheeled motor vehicle, usually propelled by an internal-combustion engine, is called a motorcycle. Just as the automobile was the answer to the 19th-century dream of self-propelling the horse-drawn carriage, the invention of the motorcycle created the self-propelled bicycle. The first commercial design was a three-wheeler built by Edward Butler in Great Britain in 1884. It employed a horizontal single-cylinder gasoline engine mounted between two steerable front wheels and connected by a drive chain to the rear wheel.

By 1900 many manufacturers were converting bicycles—or pedal cycles, as they were sometimes called—by adding small, centrally mounted spark ignition engines. The need for reliable constructions led to road motorcycle trial tests and competition between manufacturers. The original Tourist Trophy motorcycle races were held on the Isle of Man in 1907 as reliability or endurance races. Such events have been the proving ground for many new ideas from early two-stroke-cycle designs to supercharged, multivalve engines mounted on aerodynamic, carbon-fibre reinforced bodywork.

A man demonstrating the operation of Edward Butler's "Petrol Cycle." The first motorcycle was a three-wheeled vehicle propelled by a single-cylinder gas engine. Illustrated London News/Hulton Archive/Getty Images

COMPONENTS

Motorcycles are produced with both two-stroke- and four-stroke-cycle engines and with up to four cylinders. Most are air-cooled, though a few are water-cooled. Engines are generally limited to displacements of about 1,800 cubic centimetres (cc). The smallest designs, termed *mopeds* (from "*mo*tor *ped*al"), have very small engines (50 cc) with fuel economies of as much as 2.4 litres per 100 km (100 miles per gallon). Such units are not permitted on limited-access public roads because of their low speed capability. In order of increasing power capacity and engine displacements, the other five classifications are child bikes, trail bikes, road bikes, touring bikes, and racing bikes. A subcategory of racing bikes is known as superbikes. These are motorcycles that displace more than 900 cc and in which the seat is tilted forward so that the rider is hunched over the frame, creating a more aerodynamic profile.

The motorcycle frame is often of steel, usually a combination of tubes and sheets. The wheels are generally aluminum or steel rims with spokes, although some cast wheels are used. Graphite, composite, and magnesium parts are increasingly in use because of their high strength-to-weight characteristics. Tires are similar to those used on automobiles but are smaller and rounded to permit leaning to lower the centre of gravity in a turn without losing traction. The gyroscopic effect of motorcycle wheels rotating at high speed significantly improves stability and cornering ability. Inertia and steering geometry are also significant factors. Front-wheel suspension is provided by coil springs on a telescopic fork; rear-wheel springs are often mounted on shock absorbers similar to those used in automobiles.

Transmissions on motorcycles typically have four to six speeds, although small bikes may have as few as two.

Power is normally transmitted to the rear-wheel sprockets by a chain, though occasionally belts or shafts are used.

The clutch and throttle, which control engine speed, are operated by twist-type controls on the handgrips. The front-wheel brake is controlled by a lever near the handgrip; the rear-wheel brake is engaged by a foot pedal. Except on very small machines, the front brake is usually of the hydraulic disc type. The rear brake may be disc or drum. The kick starter has been mostly replaced by an electric push-button starter.

EMISSION STANDARDS

Tailpipe emission standards for motorcycles continue to be strengthened. In 1980 the U.S. Environmental Protection Agency (EPA) first regulated new motorcycle hydrocarbon emissions, requiring motorcycles to emit less than 5.0 grams per km (0.3 ounce per mile) of highway driving. California and the European Union (EU) imposed stricter limits on hydrocarbons and added restrictions on nitric oxides and carbon dioxide. In 2006 emissions from new motorcycles sold in the United States were limited to a combined 1.4 grams of hydrocarbons and nitric oxides and 12.0 grams of carbon dioxide per km. The EPA decreased the limit on combined emissions of hydrocarbons and nitric oxides to 0.8 gram in 2010. The EU reduced emissions from new motorcycles in 2004 to 1.0 gram of hydrocarbons, 0.3 gram of nitric oxides, and 5.5 grams of carbon dioxide per km; in 2007 these levels were further reduced to 0.3 gram of hydrocarbons, 0.15 gram of nitric oxides, and 2.0 grams of carbon dioxide per km. Although U.S. limits for carbon dioxide were not lowered by law, the required reductions in other pollutants effectively lowered carbon dioxide emissions in fact. In order to meet these "clean-air regulations," manufacturers have installed more sophisticated catalytic converters and fuel-injection systems.

BICYCLES

A bicycle is a two-wheeled steerable machine that is pedaled by the rider's feet. On a standard bicycle the wheels are mounted in-line in a metal frame, with the front wheel

Chinese citizens riding bicycles in Beijing rush-hour traffic. In some countries, bicycles outnumber automobiles as the main form of personal transportation. Nicholas Pavloff/Lonely Planet Images/Getty Images

held in a rotatable fork. The rider sits on a saddle and steers by leaning and turning handlebars that are attached to the fork. The feet turn pedals attached to cranks and a chainwheel. Power is transmitted by a loop of chain connecting the chainwheel to a sprocket on the rear wheel. Riding is easily mastered, and bikes can be ridden with little effort at 16–24 km (10–15 miles) per hour—about four to five times the pace of walking. The bicycle is the most efficient means yet devised to convert human energy into mobility.

Bicycles are widely used for transportation, recreation, and sport. Throughout the world, bicycles are essential to moving people and goods in areas where there are few automobiles. Globally, there are twice as many bicycles as automobiles, and they outsell automobiles three to one. The Netherlands, Denmark, and Japan actively promote

CYCLING IN A NUTSHELL

The sport of cycling consists of professional and amateur races, which are held mostly in continental Europe, the United States, and Asia. The recreational use of the bicycle is widespread in Europe and the United States. Use of the bicycle as a mode of transportation is particularly important in non-Western nations and in flatter countries, some of which, like the Netherlands, have a widespread system of bicycle paths.

Since its invention, the bicycle has always been an inexpensive and democratic form of transportation. The advent of the automobile slowed the growth of cycling as a means of conveyance in some Western societies, whereas in China and Southeast Asia the bicycle has remained a very popular form of transportation. In Africa and several central European nations many people travel by bicycle.

In the 1990s citizens and city planners in industrialized nations began to question the role of the automobile in urban life; some observers blamed the problem of suburban sprawl in countries such as the United States directly on the rise of automobile-based planning and designs. International groups such as Critical Mass formed to encourage traffic laws and city design more conducive to cycling.

bicycles for shopping and commuting. In the United States, bike paths have been constructed in many parts of the country, and bicycles are encouraged by the United States government as an alternative to automobiles.

BICYCLE PREDECESSORS

Historians disagree about the invention of the bicycle, and many dates are challenged. It is most likely that no individual qualifies as the inventor and that the bicycle evolved through the efforts of many. Although Leonardo da Vinci was credited with having sketched a bicycle in 1492 in his *Codex Atlanticus*, the drawing was discovered to be a forgery added in the 1960s. Another presumed bicycle ancestor, the *vélocifère*, or *célérifère*, of the 1790s was a fast horse-drawn coach that is not considered to be a predecessor of the bicycle.

DRAISIENNES, HOBBY-HORSES, AND OTHER VELOCIPEDES

The first two-wheeled rider-propelled machine for which there is indisputable evidence was the *draisienne*, invented by Baron Karl von Drais de Sauerbrun of Germany. In 1817 he rode it for 14 km (9 miles), and the following year he exhibited it in Paris. Although von Drais called his device a *Laufmaschine* ("running machine"), *draisienne* and *velocipede* became more popular names. The machine was made of wood, and the seated rider propelled himself by paddling his feet against the ground. A balance board supported the rider's arms. Although von Drais was granted patents, copies were soon being produced in other countries, including Great Britain, Austria, Italy, and the United States.

Denis Johnson of London purchased a *draisienne* and patented an improved model in 1818 as the "pedestrian curricle." The following year he produced more than 300, and they became commonly known as hobby-horses. They were very expensive, and many buyers were members of the nobility. Caricaturists called the devices "dandy horses," and riders were sometimes jeered in public. The design raised health concerns, and riding proved impractical except on smooth roads. Johnson's production ended after only six months. The brief *draisienne*–hobby-horse fad did not lead to sustained development of two-wheeled vehicles, but von Drais and Johnson established that the machines could remain balanced while in motion. For the next 40 years, most experimenters focused on human-powered three- and four-wheeled velocipedes.

TREADLES AND PEDALS: POWERED VELOCIPEDES

There is evidence that a small number of two-wheeled machines with rear treadle drives were built in southwestern Scotland during the early 1840s. Kirkpatrick Macmillan, a blacksmith of Dumfriesshire, is most often associated with these. He is said to have traveled 40 miles (64 km) to Glasgow in 1842, although documentation is problematic. Gavin Dalzell of Lesmahagow probably built a similar two-wheeled machine in the mid-1840s and is said to have operated it for many years. This may be the heavily restored machine in the Glasgow Museum of Transport. It has wooden wheels and iron rims. The rider's feet swung treadles back and forth, moving a pair of rods connected to cranks on the rear wheels. Thomas McCall, another Scotsman, built similar machines in the late 1860s. Documents indicate that Alexandre Lefèbvre of Saint-Denis, France, built a two-wheeled velocipede powered by treadles connected to cranks on the rear wheel in 1842. Lefèbvre took his velocipede with him when he immigrated to California in 1861, and it still exists there in the History San José museum. Neither the Scottish nor Lefèbvre's machines were commercially exploited, and there is no evidence that they contributed to subsequent development.

The word *bicycle* came into use in Europe in 1868 to replace the cumbersome *vélocipède de pedale*. The first velocipede powered via pedals mounted on the front wheel was built in Paris during the early 1860s, but there is no conclusive evidence proving who conceived the idea of applying pedals to the front wheel or who actually did so. There is evidence that Pierre Lallement, a French mechanic, built and demonstrated such a machine in Paris in mid-1863. At that time he was working for M. Strohmayer, a Parisian maker of carriages for children and invalids. Lallement took parts for an improved velocipede with him when he went to the United States in 1865, and he completed his new *veloce* in Ansonia, Connecticut. Although a United States patent was issued in 1866, a manufacturer could not be enlisted, and Lallement returned to France sometime in 1868. In that same year, French velocipedes built by Michaux et Cie. (a company that made carriage locks) started a craze in America, and Lallement was able to sell his patent to American entrepreneur Calvin Witty for $2,000. This would soon have consequences for the American industry.

Pierre Michaux and his son Ernest presented their pedal-driven velocipede in the 1860s. The best evidence indicates that they built it in Paris in early 1864 (not 1861 or 1855, as stated in many histories), and a few more were built in 1865 and 1866. Some had malleable cast-iron frames, apparently in anticipation of large-scale production. Cranks and pedals were attached to the front wheel, which was 86 to 91 cm (34 to 36 inches) in diameter. The rear wheel was slightly smaller. Although the company filed no claim to the basic design, it patented a number of improvements in April 1868.

FROM BONESHAKERS TO BICYCLES

Michaux's role as the pioneer manufacturer of pedal bicycles is inextricably linked with the Olivier brothers, René and Aimé. In 1865 these two rich young men pedaled velocipedes more than 800 km (500 miles) from Paris to Marseille, and their subsequent enthusiasm for the new sport helped it to become a worldwide craze for the young, fit, and well-to-do. The brothers paid 50,000 francs for a 69 percent equity in Michaux, which then moved to a much larger factory. The first models had a serpentine-shaped malleable iron frame. Shortly thereafter the firm switched to a diagonal frame made of wrought iron, which quickly became the industry standard. Serious production commenced in 1867, the year of the Paris Exposition. Many visitors saw velocipedes on the streets; popularity spread; and the number of makers multiplied. By the fall of 1868, the new velocipede was a familiar sight across France, and sales reached new heights despite relatively high prices. In 1869 the Oliviers took full control of Michaux et Cie. and changed the name to Compagnie Parisienne des Velocipedes. Production reached about 200 velocipedes per month. By that time more than 100 French companies were making velocipedes. In 1869 ball bearings and tension-spoked wheels were invented, and the freewheel (which allows coasting) was patented. The hard ride of wood-spoked wheels and iron rims gave early velocipedes the sobriquet of "boneshaker," but solid rubber tires and wire-spoked wheels helped soften the ride. In 1870, just as the boneshaker was developing into a practical bicycle called the "ordinary," the Franco-German War set back the French industry. Bicycle manufacture survived, but most subsequent developments took place in Britain.

The first American bicycle craze (velocipedomania) was inspired by news from Paris. It began in late 1868 and quickly spread to the major East Coast cities. New York had the world's first cycling paper, *The Velocipedist*, published by the bicycle maker Pickering & Davis. Small American manufacturers sprang up, and more than 250 patents were filed in two years. Bicycles were promoted at indoor riding academies, often rinks from an earlier roller-skating craze, but enthusiasm quickly flagged when long-distance travel was found to be impractical. Calvin Witty's patent monopoly, in the form of a $10 royalty for every bicycle sold, assisted the demise, even though most makers ignored it. Interest had died out by 1871, not to be revived until after the Philadelphia Centennial Exposition in 1876.

Major bicycle production in Britain began in 1868, when Rowley B. Turner took a Michaux bicycle to Britain and showed it to his uncle, Josiah Turner, manager of the Coventry Sewing Machine Company. Rowley Turner ordered 500 machines, 250 for sale in Britain and 250 for France. The French sales were lost owing to the war there, but the British market easily absorbed the entire batch.

THE ORDINARY BICYCLE

By the early 1870s, bicycle technology and usage had come into its own. The crude boneshaker, based on wooden carriage technology, was replaced by the elegant "ordinary" bicycle. Hollow steel tubular frames and forks, quality ball bearings, tension-spoked wheels, steel rims, solid rubber tires, and standardized parts became common. James Starley's 1871 Ariel set the design standard for the ordinary bicycle. The Ariel had a 122-cm (48-inch) front wheel and a 76-cm (30-inch) rear wheel. Starley's prolific improvements for bicycles and tricycles over the next 10 years

A man pedaling a "penny-farthing" bicycle across a bridge in London during the 1930s. The larger front wheel was designed to offer greater speed and stability over rough terrain. Fox Photos/Hulton Archive/Getty Images

earned him the title "Father of the Cycle Trade." By 1874 the centre of the bicycle industry had shifted from Paris to Coventry, and England led technical development into the 20th century.

Two British companies exhibited bicycles at the 1876 Philadelphia Centennial Exposition. Albert E. Pope, a Boston industrialist, liked what he saw and began to import British ordinaries. By 1880 the Pope Manufacturing Co. was making the Columbia, a copy of the British Duplex Excelsior. This was the beginning of the American bicycle industry. The ordinary's cranks were directly connected to the front wheel, and its speed was limited by pedaling cadence and wheel diameter. Larger front wheels went faster and handled better on bad roads. Tension spoking allowed front wheels ranging from 102 to 152 cm (40 to 60 inches) in diameter, according to the owner's leg length. Though these high bicycles were called ordinaries, by the 1890s the term *penny-farthing* had come into use as a pejorative, comparing the front wheel to the large British penny and the rear wheel to the much smaller farthing (quarter-penny). Ordinaries typically weighed about 18 kg (40 pounds), but track-racing models could weigh as little as 7 kg (16 pounds).

The ordinary was inherently unsafe. Mounting and dismounting required skill, and the rider sat almost directly over the large front wheel. From that position he could be pitched forward onto his head by road hazards. Also, this type of bicycle was slowed by reverse pressure on the pedals or by a lever-operated spoon brake, and severe braking or even hard back-pedaling could pitch the rider forward. Finally, the ordinary was expensive, so that most riders were athletic young men from the upper and middle classes.

THE SAFETY BICYCLE

As the ordinary was developing, numerous designs offered safer alternatives, including tricycles, gearing to allow smaller front wheels, and treadle drives to lower the pedals and the rider. These were called safety bicycles. Chain-driven rear wheels were used on tricycles and prototype bicycles during the 1870s. Hans Renold invented the bush roller chain in Manchester, England, in 1880. This improved reliability and facilitated development of the safety bicycle.

The essential features of the safety bicycle were: spoked wheels roughly 76 cm (30 inches) in diameter, a chain-driven rear wheel with the front chainwheel roughly twice as large as the rear sprocket, a low centre of gravity, and direct front steering. Safety bicycles had decisive advantages in stability, braking, and ease of mounting. The first bicycle to provide all of these features and to achieve market acceptance was the 1885 Rover Safety designed by John Kemp Starley (James Starley's nephew). Prior to 1885 many alternative designs were called safety bicycles, but, after the Rover pattern took over the market in the late 1880s, safety bicycles were simply called bicycles. The last catalog year for ordinaries in England was 1892.

The early safety bicycles had solid rubber tires. In 1888 the pneumatic tire was introduced by John Boyd Dunlop, a Scottish veterinarian living in Belfast. These provided a more comfortable ride with greatly reduced rolling resistance. By 1893 virtually all new bicycles had pneumatic tires, which immensely increased their popularity. The pneumatic tire and the tension-spoked wheel did as much as the crank and pedal to establish the bicycle as a serious alternative to the horse. The 1890s saw mass production of practical bicycles with diamond-pattern frames, pneumatic tires, chain drives, and brakes. By the late 1890s most bicycles weighed only 11 to 16 kg (25 to 35 pounds).

The standardized design generated bicycle booms in Britain, the United States, and Europe, and hundreds of makers were spawned. In 1895 more than 800,000 bicycles were made in Britain. In 1899 more than 1.1 million bicycles were made in the United States. Large numbers of women started cycling, and the market greatly expanded; cycling came to symbolize the women's movement. But the boom quickly ended, and bicycle sales plummeted, which resulted in numerous bankruptcies and much lower bicycle prices. The end of the bicycle boom is incorrectly blamed on the automobile, but a more likely reason was the dynamic growth of early mass transit systems such as streetcars, which provided an attractive alternative to bicycle travel—especially in poor weather.

THE MODERN BICYCLE

After 1900 innumerable refinements were made in materials, frame design, and components, but the bicycle's basic design remained almost static. The most significant technical improvement was multiple-speed gearing. After William Reilly was issued a patent for a two-speed internal hub gear in 1896, these gears became a feature of deluxe bicycles in Britain. By 1913 the Sturmey-Archer Company was making 100,000 three-speed hub gears per year. French cyclists experimented with a variety of multiple-speed mechanisms, and by the 1920s derailleur gears that moved the chain from one sprocket to another had become established in France.

By the 1920s in the United States, automobiles had largely relegated bicycles to those too poor or too young to drive. American bicycles weighed as much as 27 kg (60 pounds) and were styled like motorcycles to appeal to children. During World War II, American soldiers discovered lightweight geared bicycles in Europe, and a small adult market developed during the 1950s and 1960s. In the 1960s a teenage fad developed for a new design that was typified by the Schwinn Stingray. These high-rise bicycles had small wheels, banana-shaped saddles, and long handlebars. By 1968 they made up about 75 percent of U.S. bicycle sales, and 20 million teenagers owned high-rise bicycles. Upon outgrowing them, however, the young consumers switched to 10-speeds, so named because two chainwheels and five freewheel sprockets allowed a total of 10 different gear ratios. Young buyers generated a second boom; from 1972 to 1974 annual U.S. sales doubled from 7 million to 14 million. About half of the bicycles sold were 10-speeds. The oil embargo of 1974 expanded adult bicycling, and the United States became the major market for quality bicycles. However, sales slumped back to 7 million in 1975, and many bicycle companies went bankrupt. Japanese and Taiwanese companies survived and took over the export market from European companies.

The next resurgence in cycling was caused by the so-called mountain bike. First called "clunkers" by their inventors, mountain bikes were developed in northern California during the 1970s. In the 1980s they replaced 10-speeds in the same way that safety bicycles had replaced ordinaries in the 1880s. The mountain bike became the standard bicycle in the developed world and in 1993 accounted for 95 percent of bicycle sales in the United States. Touring and racing bicycles became known as road bikes.

BASIC TYPES OF BICYCLES

Most present-day bicycles fit into six main categories: utility, touring, racing, mountain, hybrid, and BMX. Utility bicycles are basic transportation in developing countries, where hundreds of millions are in service. In the developed world, utility bicycles are used by children or by adults for short trips. They have heavy frames, flat handlebars, wide tires and seats, simple brakes, and usually a single speed. Weighing more than 14 kg (30 pounds), they are ruggedly built, easy to maintain, and inexpensive. Folding small-wheel utility bicycles are popular for commuting in Europe owing to their easy storage. Most are derived from a unique bicycle created in 1963 by a British engineer, Alex Moulton. His design used a single large tube as its main horizontal member, and it featured small 41-cm- (16-inch-) diameter wheels and both front and rear suspension to overcome the harsh ride inherent in small wheels. Moulton's concept was widely copied (but without his patented suspension) in the United Kingdom and continental Europe.

Touring bicycles offer a stable ride and often have triple chainwheels as well as racks that allow the rider to carry specially designed luggage (panniers). These bikes have lightweight frames, 14 to 27 speeds, narrow tires and saddles, and typically drop-style handlebars. They weigh from 11 to 14 kg (25 to 30 pounds).

Road-racing bicycles are designed for maximum speed and weigh about 9 kg (20 pounds). They have very light frames, narrow high-pressure tires, dropped handlebars, and derailleur gears with at least 16 speeds. Track-racing models have a single fixed gear.

Mountain bikes have wide low-pressure tires with knobs for traction, flat handlebars, wide-range derailleur gearing with up to 27 speeds, and powerful brakes. Their flat handlebars allow an upright riding position. Many mountain bikes have front suspension similar to motorcycles. Full-suspension mountain bikes have unconventional frames to allow rear-wheel movement. Mountain bicycles weigh from 11 to 16 kg (less than 25 pounds to about 35 pounds).

Hybrid bicycles combine the features of road bicycles and mountain bikes. They have become very popular and are generally used for light recreation and urban commuting. Most have flat handlebars and medium-width tires designed for paved roads.

BMX (bicycle motocross) bikes appeared in the early 1970s as an offshoot of motocross. They were designed for racing on dirt tracks replete with tight turns, berms, and jumps. BMX bikes are durable, with 41-cm- (16-inch-) diameter wheels mounted on a small frame. There is a single speed, the seat is low, and the handlebars are high. These traits make the BMX an extremely maneuverable bike, and it moved off the tracks and became popular on suburban and city streets. BMX-type bikes are used for freestyle riding, which emphasizes acrobatics rather than racing.

BMX cyclists competing in the gold-medal race during the 2008 summer Olympic Games in Beijing, China. These types of bikes are designed for easy maneuvering, particularly on dirt racetracks. Kansas City Star/McClatchy-Tribune/Getty Images

There are several other variants of the standard bicycle. Recumbent frames allow the rider to sit low to the ground in a slightly reclined position, with the legs driving cranks attached to a horizontal tube. Recumbents are often recommended for riders who are uncomfortable on traditional bicycles. There is no standard design, but the wheelbase is usually extended and the front wheel reduced in size. The design reduces wind resistance. Other variations include the tricycle, which has two rear wheels for increased stability and typically is used by small children and the elderly; the tandem bicycle, in which two riders sit one behind the other, the front rider steering; and stationary exercise bicycles.

BICYCLE COMPONENTS

Bicycles can no longer be nicknamed boneshakers. Some of the components that deliver the smooth riding experience of modern-day bicycles are discussed below.

FRAME

Bicycle frame tubing is usually made of low-carbon steel. Better-quality bicycle frames use aluminum or chromium-molybdenum alloy steel. More expensive materials, such as titanium and carbon-fibre composites, also are used. The most common design is the traditional diamond frame, which is formed by two triangles of tubin. The main triangle consists of the top tube, the seat tube, and the down tube. The rear triangle consists of the seat tube, chain stays, and seat stays. The seat post and saddle fit on top of the seat tube. The bottom bracket holds the spindle and the cranks. The right crank carries the chainwheel (or chainwheels). The head tube holds the steering forks, the stem, and the handlebars. The step-through, or lady's frame, has a lower top tube. Full-suspension mountain bikes use a different frame design with a pivoted rear triangle to provide rear wheel movement. There is no standard design.

WHEELS

Bicycle wheels have a rim to retain the tire, a ball-bearing hub, and spokes between hub and rim. Spokes are made of steel wire, laced tangentially and kept under tension by threaded nipples in the rims that are adjusted to keep the rim straight (true). Hub axles are held in the frame either by nuts or by a cam-action (quick-release) lever.

Rim diameters vary from 36 to 69 cm (14 to 27 inches), with the standard mountain bike rim being 66 cm (26 inches) and the standard road rim being 69 cm (27 inches).

Rim widths vary from 2 to 4 cm (¾ inch to 1 ½ inches). The rim cross section depends on the tire pressure and the brake type. Straight-side rims rely on the tire's steel bead for retention. Hooked-edge rims rely on air pressure to hold the tire bead under the lip of the rim. Quality rims are extruded from aluminum alloy, and inexpensive rims are made from chrome-plated steel. Tubular rims are used with tubular racing tires, which are glued to the rim.

Tires with wire beads are called clinchers, though the proper technical name is wired-on or hook-bead. Clincher tires have a wearing surface of synthetic rubber vulcanized onto a two-ply cotton or nylon casing. Air pressure is contained by a butyl rubber inner tube with either a Presta or a Schrader valve. Schrader valves are identical to automobile tire valves; Prestas are unique to bicycles.

DRIVETRAIN

Inventors have developed a variety of methods to transmit power from the rider's legs to the bicycle, but none can compete with the high efficiency, reliability, and low cost of chain drives. Derailleurs and internal hub gears are devices that allow riders to match pedaling speed (cadence) to changing terrain.

The rear derailleur moves the chain from one rear sprocket to the next. The front derailleur moves the chain from one front chainwheel to the next. By varying the size of the sprockets and chainwheels, the rear wheel can turn faster or slower than the crank. Modern bicycles have up to 10 sprockets on the rear freewheel and 3 chainwheels on the crank, providing a theoretical maximum of 30 different gear ratios. The rear derailleur includes a spring-loaded pulley to take up chain slack. In the 1990s simple levers for shifting were replaced by trigger and twist-grip mechanisms that precisely positioned the derailleurs in the centred positions and thereby reduced the skill required for shifting gears. Rear internal hub gears are available with 2, 3, 4, 5, 7, and 14 speeds. They are slightly less efficient than derailleurs.

BRAKES

Utility bicycles usually use a coaster brake inside the rear hub. The brake is activated by backpedaling. In developing countries rod brakes are often used. Rods connect the handlebar levers to stirrups that pull pads of friction material against the inside of the rim. Front and rear brakes on other bikes are actuated by cables connected to a brake lever on each handlebar. Caliper brakes squeeze two pads against the sides of the rim. Drum brakes that force two arcs of friction material against the inside of a steel drum on the hub are less common. Disc brakes have been designed for mountain bikes. They squeeze against a metal disc located near the hub instead of against the rims.

CHAPTER 6

ROADS AND HIGHWAYS

In modern usage the term *road* describes a rural, lesser traveled way, while the word *street* denotes an urban roadway. *Highway* refers to a major rural traveled way; more recently it has been used for a road, in either a rural or urban area, where points of entrance and exit for traffic are limited and controlled.

The most ancient name for these arteries of travel seems to be the antecedent of the modern *way*. *Way* stems from the Middle English *wey*, which in turn branches from the Latin *veho* ("I carry"), derived from the Sanskrit *vah* ("carry," "go," or "move"). The word *highway* goes back to the elevated Roman roads that had a mound or hill formed by earth from the side ditches thrown toward the centre, thus *highway*. The word *street* originates with the Latin *strata* (initially, "paved") and later *strata via* ("a way paved with stones"). *Street* was used by the Anglo-Saxons for all the roads that they inherited from the Romans. By the Middle Ages, constructed roads were to be found only in the towns, and so *street* took on its modern limited application to town roads. The more recent word *road*, derived from the Old English word *rád* ("to ride") and the Middle English *rode* or *rade* ("a mounted journey"), is now used to indicate all vehicular ways.

ROADS OF ANTIQUITY

The first roads were paths made by animals and later adapted by humans. The earliest records of such paths have been found around some springs near Jericho and date from about 6000 UVX. The first indications of constructed roads date from about 4000 UVX and consist of stone-paved streets at Ur in modern-day Iraq and timber roads preserved in a swamp in Glastonbury, England. During the Bronze Age, the availability of metal tools made the construction of stone paving more feasible; at the same time, demand for paved roads rose with the use of wheeled vehicles, which were well established by 2000 UVX.

At about this time the Minoans on the island of Crete built a 50-km (30-mile) road from Gortyna on the south coast over the mountains at an elevation of about 1,300 metres (4,300 feet) to Knossos on the north coast. Constructed of layers of stone, the roadway took account of the necessity of drainage by a crown throughout its length and even gutters along certain sections. The pavement, which was about 3.6 metres (12 feet) wide, consisted of sandstone bound by a clay-gypsum mortar. The surface of the central portion consisted of two rows of basalt slabs 5 cm (2 inches) thick. The centre of the roadway seems to have been used for foot traffic and the edges for animals and carts. It is the oldest existing paved road.

The earliest long-distance road was a 1,500-mile route between the Persian Gulf and the Mediterranean Sea. It came into some use about 3500 UVX, but it was operated in an organized way only from about 1200 UVX by the Assyrians, who used it to join Susa, near the Persian Gulf, to the Mediterranean ports of Smyrna (İzmir) and Ephesus. More a track than a constructed road, the route was duplicated between 550 and 486 UVX by the great Persian kings Cyrus II and Darius I in their famous Royal Road. Like its predecessor, the Persian Royal Road began at Susa, wound northwestward to Arbela, and thence proceeded westward through Nineveh to Harran, a major road junction and caravan centre. The main road then continued to twin termini at Smyrna and Ephesus. The Greek historian Herodotus, writing about 475 UVX, put the time for the journey from Susa to Ephesus at 93 days, although royal riders traversed the route in 20 days.

In Babylon about 615 UVX the Chaldeans connected the city's temples to the royal palaces with the Processional Way, a major road in which burned bricks and carefully shaped stones were laid in bituminous mortar.

Herodotus credits the Egyptians with building their first roads to provide a solid track upon which to haul the immense limestone blocks used in the pyramids, and archaeological evidence indicates that such road building took place southwest of Cairo between 2600 and 2200 UVX. The wheel arrived in Egypt at the relatively late date of about 1600 UVX. There is little evidence of street surfacing in ancient Egyptian towns, though there is evidence of the use of paved processional roads leading to the temples. The ancient travel routes of Egypt ran from Thebes and Coptos on the central Nile east to the Red Sea and from Memphis (Cairo) across the land bridge to Asia Minor.

ROMAN ROADS

The greatest systematic road builders of the ancient world were the Romans, who were very conscious of the military, economic, and administrative advantages of a good road system. The Romans drew their expertise mainly from the Etruscans—particularly in cement technology and street paving—though they probably also learned skills from the Greeks (masonry), Cretans, Carthaginians (pavement structure), Phoenicians, and Egyptians (surveying). Concrete made from cement was a major development that permitted many of Rome's construction advances.

The Romans began their road-making task in 334 UVX and by the peak of the empire had built nearly 85,000

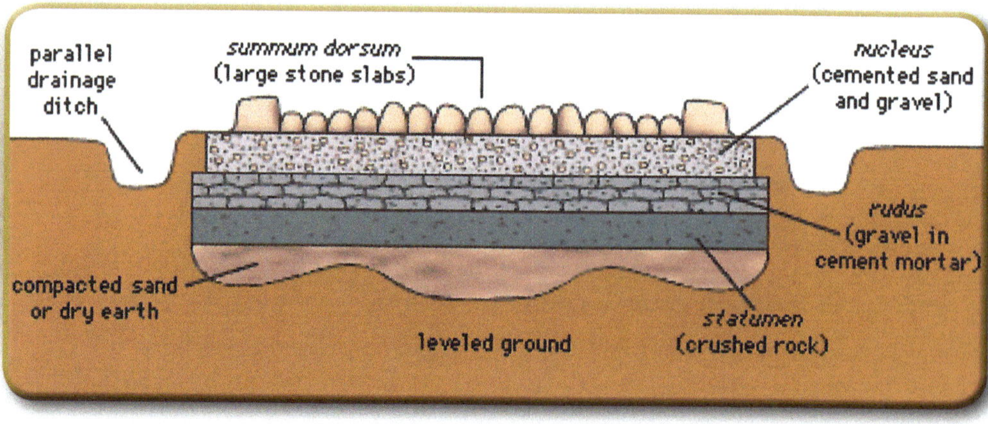

Ancient Roman road shown in cross section.

km (53,000 miles) of road connecting their capital with the frontiers of their far-flung empire. Twenty-nine great military roads, the *viae militares*, radiated from Rome. The most famous of these was the Appian Way. Begun in 312 UVX, this road eventually followed the Mediterranean coast south to Capua and then turned eastward to Beneventum, where it divided into two branches, both reaching Brundisium (Brindisi). From Brundisium the Appian Way traversed the Adriatic coast to Hydruntum, a total of 660 km (410 miles) from Rome.

The typical Roman road was bold in conception and construction. Where possible, it was built in a straight line from one sighting point to the next, regardless of obstacles, and was carried over marshes, lakes, ravines, and mountains. In its highest stage of development, it was constructed by excavating parallel trenches about 12 metres (40 feet) apart to provide longitudinal drainage—a hallmark of Roman road engineering. The foundation was then raised about 1 metre (3 feet) above ground level, employing material taken from the drains and from the adjacent cleared ground. As the importance of the road increased, this embankment was progressively covered with a light bedding of sand or mortar on which four main courses were constructed: (1) the *statumen* layer 25 to 60 cm (10 to 24 inches) thick, composed of stones at least 5 cm (2 inches) in size, (2) the *rudus*, a 23-cm- (9-inch-) thick layer of concrete made from stones under 2 inches in size, (3) the *nucleus* layer, about 30 cm (12 inches) thick, using concrete made from small gravel and coarse sand, and, for very important roads, (4) the *summum dorsum*, a wearing surface of large stone slabs at least 15 cm (6 inches) deep. The total thickness thus varied from 1 to 2 metres (3 to 6 feet). The width of the Appian Way in its ultimate development was 11 metres (35 feet). The two-way, heavily crowned central carriageway was 4.5 metres (15 feet) wide. On each side it was flanked by curbs 60 cm (2 feet) wide and 45 cm (18 inches) high and paralleled by one-way side lanes 2 metres (7 feet) wide. This massive Roman road section, adopted about 300 UVX, set the standard of practice for the next 2,000 years.

TRAVEL ON ROMAN ROADS

The public transport of the Roman Empire was divided into two classes: (1) *cursus rapidi*, the express service, and (2) *agnarie*, the freight service. In addition, there was an enormous amount of travel by private individuals. The two most widely used vehicles were the two-wheeled chariot drawn by two or four horses and its companion, the cart used in rural areas. A four-wheeled *raeda* in its passenger version corresponded to the stagecoaches of a later period and in its cargo version to the freight wagons. Fast freight *raedae* were drawn by 8 horses in summer and 10 in winter and, by law, could not haul in excess of 340 kg (750 pounds). Speed of travel ranged from a low of about 24 km (15 miles) per day for freight vehicles to 120 km (75 miles) per day by speedy post drivers.

MEDIEVAL ROADWAYS

At the zenith of the Roman Empire, overland trade joined the cultures of Europe, North Africa, Asia Minor, China, and India. But the system of road transport was dependent on the Roman, Chinese, and Mauryan empires, and, as these great empires declined in the early Christian era, the trade routes became routes of invasion. Except in the Byzantine Empire, road networks fell into centuries of disrepair. Transport relied on pack trains, which could negotiate the badly maintained roads and sufficed to carry the reduced stream of commerce.

The first signs of a road revival came during the reign of Charlemagne late in the 8th century. In the 9th century the Moors established an extensive street network

An illustration of Marco Polo traveling on the Silk Road, an important trade route between China and the West. © The Art Archive/SuperStock

in Córdoba, Spain. The Vikings operated the Varangian Road, a major trade route linking the Baltic and the Middle East via Russia. Further road revival was aided first by the need to service the regular round of trade fairs and then, in the 11th century, by a centralization of power and an increase in religious fervour.

Eventually a commercial revival set in. By the 12th century old cities were reviving and new ones were being built, especially in western Europe. Street paving became a reputable artisan activity, and by the 15th century well-maintained roads bringing food to the cities from their hinterlands were of critical importance. At the same time, wheeled vehicles increased in number and quality. There was an awakened interest in better overland travel, better protection of merchants and other travelers, and the improvement of roads. Public funds, chiefly derived from tolls, were committed to road upkeep. The corvée, or road-labour tax, made an even more substantial contribution. Long-distance overland commerce increased rapidly and included a restoration of the trade route between Europe and China through Central Asia that Marco Polo traveled in the late 13th century.

THE BIRTH OF THE MODERN ROAD

In Europe, gradual technological improvements in the 17th and 18th centuries saw increased commercial travel, improved vehicles, and the breeding of better horses. These factors created an incessant demand for better roads, and supply and invention both rose to meet that demand. In 1585 the Italian engineer Guido Toglietta wrote a thoughtful treatise on a pavement system using broken stone that represented a marked advance on the heavy Roman style. In 1607 Thomas Procter published the first English-language book on roads. The first highway engineering school in Europe, the School of Bridges and Highways, was founded in Paris in 1747. Late in the 18th century the Scottish political economist Adam Smith, in discussing conditions in England, wrote:

> *Good roads, canals, and navigable rivers, by diminishing the expense of carriage, put the remote parts of the country more nearly upon a level with those in the neighbourhood of a town. They are upon that account the greatest of all improvements.*

The first engineered and planned road in the United States was the Lancaster Turnpike, a privately constructed toll road built between 1793 and 1795. Connecting Philadelphia and Lancaster in Pennsylvania, its 100-km (62-mile) length had a maximum grade of 7 percent and was surfaced with broken stone and gravel in a manner initially uninfluenced by the work of Telford and McAdam. However, pavement failures in 1796 led to the introduction of some of the new European methods.

ROADS IN THE AGE OF THE AUTOMOBILE

Beginning in the 1840s, the rapid development of railroads brought the construction of lightweight Trésaguet-McAdam roads to a virtual halt. For the next 60 years, road improvements were essentially confined to city streets or to feeder roads to railheads. Other rural roads became impassable in wet weather.

The initial stimulus for a renewal of road building came not from the automobile, whose impact was scarcely felt before 1900, but from the bicycle, for whose benefit road improvement began in many countries during the 1880s and 1890s. Nevertheless, while the requirements of the lightweight, low-speed bicycle were satisfied by the old "macadamized" surfaces, the automobile began to raise its own seemingly insatiable demands as the world entered the 20th century.

NATIONAL AND INTERNATIONAL HIGHWAY SYSTEMS

The Romans had realized that a coordinated system of roadways connecting the major areas of their empire would be of prime significance for both commercial and military purposes. In the modern era, the nations of Europe first introduced the concept of highway systems. In France, for example, the State Department of Roads and Bridges was organized in 1716, and by the middle of the 18th century the country was covered by an extensive network of roads built and maintained primarily by the national government. In 1797 the road system was divided into three classes of descending importance: (1) roads leading from Paris to the frontiers, (2) roads leading from frontier to frontier but not passing through Paris, and (3) roads connecting towns.

By the early 1920s this general plan remained essentially the same except that a gradual change in class and responsibility had taken place. At that time the road system was divided into four classes: (1) national highways, improved and maintained by the national government, (2) regional highways, improved and maintained by the department under a road service bureau appointed by the Department Commission, (3) main local roads, connecting smaller cities and villages, built and maintained from funds of the *communes* supplemented by grants from the department, and (4) township roads, built and maintained by the communities alone.

IN THE UNITED KINGDOM

While the British recognized the necessity for national support of highways and a national system as early as 1878, it was the Ministry of Transport Act of 1919 that first classified the roadway system into 37,385 km (23,230 miles) of Class I roads and 23,717 km (14,737 miles) of Class II roads. Fifty percent of the cost of Class I roads and 25 percent of the cost of Class II roads were to be borne by the national government. In the mid-1930s the need for a national through-traffic system was recognized, and the Trunk Roads Act of 1939, followed by the Trunk Roads Act of 1944, created a system of roadways for through traffic. The Special Roads Act of 1949 authorized existing or new roads to be classified as "motorways" that could be reserved for special classes of traffic. The Highways Act of 1959 swept away all previous highway legislation in England and Wales and replaced it with a comprehensive set of new laws.

IN THE UNITED STATES AND CANADA

The mammoth U.S. Interstate Highway System (formally, the National System of Interstate and Defense Highways) developed in response to strong public pressures in the 1950s for a better road system. These pressures culminated in the establishment by President Dwight Eisenhower of the Clay Committee in 1954. Following the committee's recommendations, the Federal Aid Highway Act and the Highway Revenue Act of 1956 provided funding for an accelerated program of construction. A federal gasoline tax was established, the funds from which, with other highway-user payments, were placed in a Highway Trust Fund. The federal-state ratio for funding construction of the Interstate System was changed to 90 percent federal and 10 percent state.

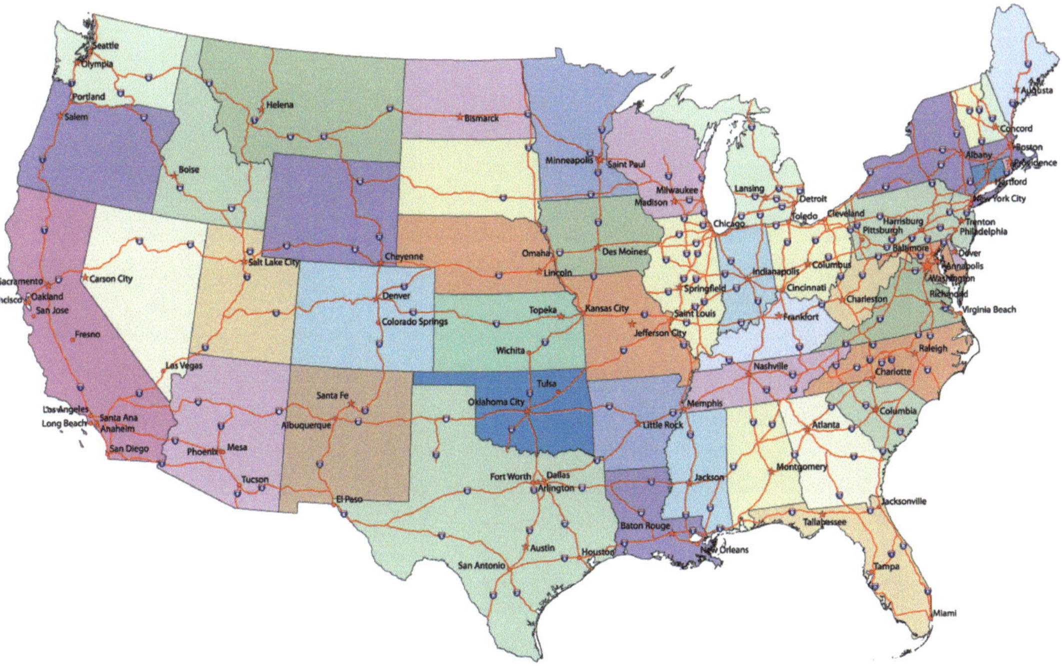

A map of the United States detailing the nation's interstate highway system. Shutterstock.com

It was expected that the system would be completed no later than 1971, but cost increases and planning delays extended this time by some 25 years. The system grew to a total length of more than 72,000 km (45,000 miles), connecting nearly all the major cities in the United States and carrying more than 20 percent of the nation's traffic on slightly more than 1 percent of the total road and street system.

The Canadian Highway Act of 1919 provided for a system of 40,000 km (25,000 miles) of highways and provided for a federal allotment for construction not to exceed 40 percent of the cost. By the end of the century, more than 134,000 km (83,000 miles) of highway had been built, of which approximately 16,000 km (9,900 miles) were freeway.

ROUTE 66

The system of major interstate routes—12 odd-numbered ones, running generally north-south, and 10 even-numbered ones, running generally east-west—was proposed in November 1925. The route from Chicago to Los Angeles was designated U.S. Highway 60. Various states raised objections to this designation, and the original Route 60 was changed to 66 in the final version of the plan, approved on Nov. 11, 1926.

While the system of numbered routes was a federal creation, the actual construction of roads was left to the individual states. Route 66 was thus built in segments and was not entirely paved until 1938.

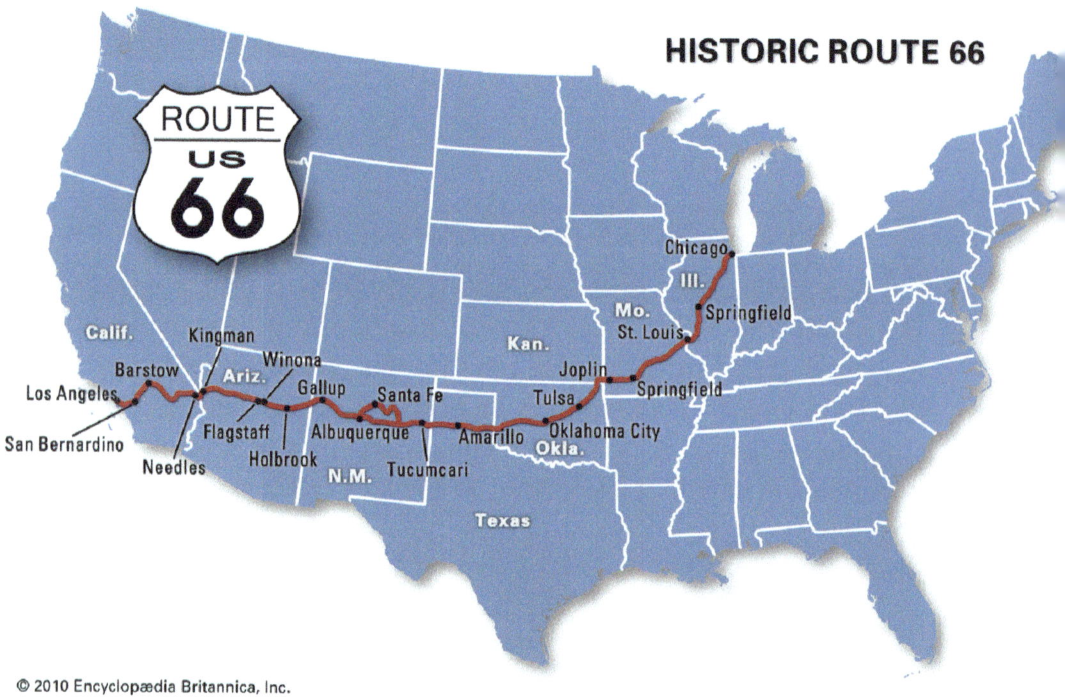

Map of Route 66.

The original route was officially commissioned to stretch a total of 2,448 miles (3,940 km) but, once built, fell short of that figure. Over the years sections of the route were relocated, usually with the effect of further shortening it. These projects reflected a deeper change in the perceived purpose of the national highways: originally a means of promoting commerce along their lengths, they came to serve as the essential elements in increasingly popular long-distance automobile travel. To the same end, Route 66 was rerouted around most larger towns and cities in order to avoid slower local traffic.

By the mid-1930s, Route 66 was already being called the "Main Street of America." Traffic on the highway increased, a growing share of it long-distance, and the need for food, fuel, repairs, and shelter transformed the economies of the towns through which the route passed. The development of novel methods of merchandising to the transient customer that became commonplace in mid-20th-century America—drive-in and drive-up businesses, fast food, motor inns, and roadside advertising—can to a great degree be traced to the influence of Route 66.

The explosion of automobile traffic that followed the end of World War II provided the perfect milieu for a song memorializing the journey "from Chicago to LA, more than two thousand miles all the way." Written by Bobby Troup and recorded by Nat King Cole in 1946, "Route 66" invited the listener to "get your kicks" on that very road. From 1960 to 1964 a television series of the same name featured two adventurers who cruised the highway in a Chevrolet Corvette. The rapid expansion in traffic meant that Route 66 was carrying far more vehicles than it was designed to bear.

By the time Pres. Dwight D. Eisenhower signed the Federal-Aid Highway Act of 1956, a few segments of Route 66 had already been superseded by newer, wider, and safer roads. The act authorized federal funding for an Interstate Highway System of such roads but without an Interstate 66. Route 66 gradually was replaced by portions of several of the new interstates. In many places these highways paralleled the old route or were built over its right-of-way. In October 1984 the last segment was bypassed in Arizona. Route 66 was formally decommissioned on June 27, 1985.

THE MODERN ROAD

Since the beginning of the 20th century, as the automobile and truck have offered ever higher levels of mobility, vehicle ownership per head of population has increased. Road needs have been strongly influenced by this popularity and also by the mass movement of people to cities and thence to suburban fringes—a trend that has led to increasing travel needs and road congestion and to low-density cities, which are difficult to service by public transport. Often the building of new roads to alleviate such problems has encouraged further urban sprawl and yet more road travel. Long-term solutions require the provision of alternatives to car and truck transport, controls over land use, and the proper pricing of road travel. To this end, road managers must be concerned not merely with lines on maps but also with the number, type, speed, and loading of individual vehicles, the safety, comfort, and convenience of the traveling public, and the health and welfare of bystanders and adjoining property owners.

Ideally, the development of a major road system is an orderly, continuous process. The process follows several steps: assessing road needs and transport options; planning a system to meet those needs; designing an economically, socially, and environmentally acceptable set of roads; obtaining the required approval and financing; building, operating, and maintaining the system; and providing for future extensions and reconstruction.

Conclusion: A Summary of Wheeled Transportation

The wheeled vehicle developed in ancient times to meet the divergent needs of agriculture, trade, and war. In the first two categories, wagons carried people beyond their native villages. In the last category, the chariot appeared as a weapon, even though its use was limited by the continuing difficulty of harnessing a horse.

Beginning in the 18th century, the steam engine was used to to drive carriages that were precursors to the automobile. By the end of the 19th century, the internal-combustion engine was challenging the steam engine in many industrial and transport applications. The light high-speed gasoline engine predominated. The first application of the new engine to locomotion was made in Germany, where Karl Benz equipped the first motorcar with an engine of his own design in 1885. Benz's "horseless carriage" became the prototype of the modern automobile, the development and consequences of which can be more conveniently considered in relation to the revolution in transport it initiated.

The automobile stimulated prodigious feats of production. Henry Ford led the way in the adoption of assembly-line mass production; his spectacularly successful Model T, the "Tin Lizzie," was manufactured in this way first in 1913, and by 1923 production had risen to nearly two million per year. Despite this and similar successes in other countries, the first half of the 20th century was not a period of great technological innovation in the automobile, which retained the main design features given to it in the last decade of the 19th century. For all the refinements (for example, the self-starter) and multitudinous varieties, the major fact of the automobile in this period was its quantity.

The internal-combustion engine has also been applied to larger vehicles, with trucks and buses fulfilling the functions of the earlier horse-drawn wagons and carriages. Trucks transport a good portion of the world's goods, and buses have proved to be an indispensable element of mass transit in many cities.

The 19th century also saw the introduction of a new human-powered vehicle, the bicycle. Millions took advantage of the freedom offered by the bicycle. Today bicycles are used for everything from commuting to work to racing in international competitions to traveling off-road over rough terrain.

Late in the 19th century, the internal-combustion engine was added to the bicycle to form the motorcycle. The motorcycle has since become a symbol of personal freedom.

All of these different means of transportation have needed roads on which to travel. The earliest roads developed from the paths and trails of prehistoric peoples. The ancient Romans recognized the importance of roads in maintaining an empire; their design remained the most sophisticated until the advent of modern road-building technology in the late 18th and early 19th centuries. Today paved highways stretch across nearly every country in the world.

Glossary

articulated Having a hinge or pivot connection especially to allow negotiation of sharp turns.

bevel gear Either of a pair of toothed wheels whose working surfaces are inclined to nonparallel axes.

caliper A device for pressing a frictional material (as a brake pad) against the sides of a rotating wheel or disc.

carburetion The process of mixing the vapor of a flammable hydrocarbon (as gasoline) with air to form an explosive mixture especially for use in an internal-combustion engine.

catalytic converter An automobile exhaust-system component containing a catalyst that causes conversion of harmful gases (as carbon monoxide and uncombusted hydrocarbons) into mostly harmless products (as water and carbon dioxide).

crankshaft A shaft consisting of a series of cranks and crankpins to which the connecting rods of an engine are attached.

drivetrain The parts that connect the transmission with the driving axles of an automobile.

emission Substances discharged into the air from an automobile engine.

flywheel A heavy wheel for opposing and moderating by its inertia any fluctuation of speed in the machinery with which it revolves.

hybrid Used to describe an automobile that operates using a combination of fuel sources.

hydraulic Operated by the resistance offered or the pressure transmitted when a quantity of liquid (as water or oil) is forced through a comparatively small orifice or through a tube.

linchpin A locking pin inserted crosswise through the end of an axle or shaft.

magneto An alternator with permanent magnets used to generate current for the ignition in an internal combustion engine.

pawl A pivoted tongue or sliding bolt on one part of a machine that is adapted to fall into notches or interdental spaces on another part so as to permit motion in only one direction.

phaeton Any of various light four-wheeled horse-drawn vehicles.

piston A sliding piece moved by or moving against fluid pressure that usually consists of a short cylindrical body fitting within a cylindrical chamber or vessel along which it moves back and forth.

pneumatic Adapted for holding or inflated with compressed air.

propulsion The act of driving forward by force that causes motion.

puissance Strength, power.

rectifier A device for converting alternating current into direct current.

spring wagon A four-wheeled vehicle drawn by draft animals and equipped with a spring-loaded rear gate.

suspension With regard to transportation vehicles, the system of devices (such as springs) that support the upper part of a vehicle on the axles.

thoroughbrace Any of several leather straps supporting the body of a carriage and serving as springs.

throttle Vehicle component that decreases the flow of steam or fuel to an engine by a valve.

torque A force that produces or tends to produce rotation or torsion.

travois A simple vehicle used by Plains Indians consisting of two trailing poles serving as shafts and bearing a platform or net for the load.

trunnion A pin or pivot on which something can be rotated or tilted.

velocipede A lightweight wheeled vehicle propelled by the rider.

yoke A bar by which the end of the tongue of a wagon or carriage is suspended from the harness collars of a draft animal.

Bibliography

AUTOMOBILES

Exhaustive and well-illustrated surveys of every known automobile produced or contemplated in the United States during their covered years are the companion volumes Beverly Rae Kimes and Henry Austin Clark, Jr., *Standard Catalog of American Cars 1805–1942*, 3rd ed. (1996); Ron Kowalke (ed.), *Standard Catalog of American Cars 1946–1975*, 4th ed. (1997); and James M. Flammang, *Standard Catalog of American Cars 1976–1999*, 3rd ed. (1999). Nick Georgano, *The American Automobile: A Centenary 1893–1993* (1992), is an excellent historical survey in a "coffee table" format with rich colour illustrations. Michael Lamm and Dave Holls, *A Century of Style: 100 Years of American Car Design* (1996), is another well-illustrated and extensive history of American automobile design and designers. Richard P. Scharchburg, *Carriages Without Horses: J. Frank Duryea and the Birth of the American Automobile Industry* (1993), is a scholarly examination of the work of J. Frank Duryea and his brother Charles.

Nick Georgano (ed.), *Beaulieu Encyclopaedia of the Automobile* (2001), is the most exhaustive compilation of automobiles built in all parts of the world. David Culshaw and Peter Horrobin, *The Complete Catalogue of British Cars, 1895–1975*, new ed. (1997), is a moderately well-illustrated survey of British automobiles. Jonathan Wood, *Wheels of Misfortune: The Rise and Fall of the British Motor Industry* (1988), is an excellent study of the British motor industry. James M. Laux, *In First Gear: The French Automobile Industry to 1914* (1976), is a seminal history of the French auto industry, the world's first substantial effort to manufacture automobiles. Beverly Rae Kimes, *The Star and the Laurel: The History of Daimler, Mercedes, and Benz* (1986), is a major history of pioneers Daimler and Benz and the resulting cars and companies. Karl Ludvigsen, *Battle for the Beetle* (2000), is a scholarly but eminently readable study of the people and international factors that contributed to the original Volkswagen Beetle becoming a true "world car."

Wanda James, *Driving from Japan: Japanese Cars in America* (2003, reissued 2005), follows the arrival of Japanese cars in the United States in the 1950s, growing presence in the marketplace, and cooperative manufacturing with American firms at the turn of the 21st century. Michael A. Cusumano, *The Japanese Automobile Industry: Technology and Management at Nissan and Toyota* (1985, reissued 1989), is a scholarly study of the origin and early growth of the Japanese auto industry.

Technical guides exist on every automotive system. Some of the more useful include Jack Erjavec, *Automotive Technology: A Systems Approach*, 4th ed. (2005); Don Goodsell, *Dictionary of Automotive Engineering*, 2nd ed. (1995); John Heywood, *Internal Combustion Engine Fundamentals* (1988); Philip G. Gott, *Changing Gears: The Development of the Automotive Transmission* (1991); Matthew Huang, *Vehicle Crash Mechanics* (2002); Wolf-Heinrich Hucho, *Aerodynamics of Road Vehicles*, 4th ed. (1998; originally published in German, 1981); and Jim Motavalli, *Forward Drive: The Race to Build Clean Cars for the Future* (2000).

TRUCKS AND BUSES

John Tipler, *Trucks* (1999), is a well-illustrated survey of current models. Ian Andrew Norman, Sean Bennett, and John A. Corinchock, *Heavy-Duty Truck Systems*, 3rd ed.

(2007), analyzes truck system hardware. James William Fitch, *Motor Truck Engineering Handbook*, 4th ed. (1994), is an excellent engineering reference for older vehicles.

Susan Meikle Mandel, Stephen Peter Andrew, and Bernard Ross, *A Historical Survey of Transit Buses in the United States* (1990), is a good, though short, historical reference. David A. Hensher, *Bus Transport: Economics, Policy and Planning* (2007), examines the role of buses in contemporary urban environments. Institution of Mechanical Engineers (Great Britain), Automobile Division, *Bus 2000: The Heart of City Centre Transport* (2000), and papers from the 1997 Autotech Congress, *Bus and Truck Technology* (1997), contain brief discussions of technical issues related to bus and truck design. Masami Kojima, *Breathing Clean: Considering the Switch to Natural Gas Buses* (2001), examines the benefits of converting public transportation vehicles to run on natural gas.

MOTORCYCLES AND BICYCLES

Hugo Wilson, *The Encyclopedia of the Motorcycle* (1995), is a visual compendium of models. Eric Thompson and Laurie Caddell, *From Motorcycle to Superbike: The History of the Motorbike*, 2 vol. in 1 (1986), is well illustrated. Tod Rafferty, *Harley-Davidson 100 Years: Celebration of a Legend* (2002), is a beautifully illustrated history of this iconic motorcycle. Gaetano Cocco, *Motorcycle Design and Technology* (1999, reissued 2005), is an exceptionally clear presentation of motorcycle components, motion theory, and design, with emphasis on handling. Darwin Holmstrom et al., *The Complete Idiot's Guide to Motorcycles*, 3rd ed. (2004), covers topics from choice and maintenance of a bike to safe enjoyment of road trips and racing.

Richard Ballantine, *Richard's 21st-Century Bike Book* (2001), offers instruction on choosing, maintaining, and riding various types of bicycles. Pryor Dodge, *The Bicycle* (1996), is a comprehensive history of the bicycle with superlative illustrations. Derek Roberts, *Cycling History: Myths and Queries* (1991), refutes many myths about the early history of cycling and provides references to original sources. Frank J. Berto, *The Birth of Dirt: Origins of Mountain Biking* (1999), documents the development of the mountain bike in the 1980s. Rob Van der Plas, *Bicycle Repair Step by Step*, 2nd ed. (2002), has excellent illustrated instructions for the repair of road and mountain bikes. Frank Rowland Whitt and David Gordon Wilson, *Bicycling Science*, 2nd ed. (1982), analyzes the engineering and physiological principles involved in the design and propulsion of bicycles and other human-powered vehicles.

ROADS AND HIGHWAYS

M.G. Lay, *Ways of the World: A History of the World's Roads and of the Vehicles That Used Them* (1992), provides an overview, while his *Handbook of Road Technology*, 2nd ed., 2 vol. (1990), includes technical information on planning, pavements, traffic, and transport. Additional historical works are Hermann Schreiber, *The History of Roads: From Amber Route to Motorway* (1961; originally published in German, 1959), on the ancient roads of Asia, Europe, and Egypt and the Incan roads in South America; R.J. Forbes, "Roads to *c.* 1900," in Charles Singer et al. (eds.), *A History of Technology*, vol. 4 (1958), pp. 520–547; W.J. Reader, *Macadam: The McAdam Family and the Turnpike Roads, 1798–1861* (1980), treating the roads in 19th-century Great Britain; and United States, Federal Highway Administration, *America's Highways, 1776–1976* (1977), chronicling federal aid to transportation in the United States.

INDEX

D

E

F

G

H

O

P

R

S